MAKE YOUR OWN LONDON LANDMARKS

MAKE YOUR OWN LONDON LANDMARKS

5 MODELS KEITH FINCH TO CONSTRUCT

Thames & Hudson

First published in the United Kingdom in 2014 by
Thames & Hudson Ltd, 181A High Holborn,
London WC1V 7QX

Paper engineering, text, design and layout © 2014 BlueRed Press Ltd
Paper engineering Keith Finch
Model illustration by Insight Design Concept Ltd

Picture Credits:
All photography of the models © 2014 BlueRed Press Ltd
All other photography from Shutterstock:
p6, 7 (L—R) pisaphotography, Eddy Galeotti, Bikeworldtravel, Bikeworldtravel, FER737NG,
Ilia Torlin, TungCheung, chrisdorney, Luciano Mortula, Dutourdumonde Photography,
p8 Matt Gibson, p9 Vinicius Tupinamba, p10 olavs, p11 (top) Eddy Galeotti,
p11 (bottom) Ilia Torlin, p16/17 Michelle Dulieu, p18 (top) Andrei Nekrassov, p18 (bottom)
Bikeworldtravel, p19 Luciano Mortula, p24 TungCheung, p25 pisaphotography,
p26 vichie81, p27 (top) Kiev.Victor, p27 (bottom) FER737NG, p32 pisaphotography,
p33 chrisdorney, p34 Dutourdumonde Photography, p35 (top) Alexandra Thompson,
p35 (bottom) Mr Pics, p40 clearlens, p41 Luciano Mortula, p42 Apurva Madia, p43 (top)
chrisdorney, p43 (bottom) Bikeworldtravel

British Library Cataloguing-in-Publication Data
A catalogue record for this book is available from the British Library

ISBN 978-0-500-51754-3

Printed and bound in China

To find out about all our publications, please visit **www.thamesandhudson.com**.
There you can subscribe to our e-newsletter, browse or download our current catalogue,
and buy any titles that are in print.

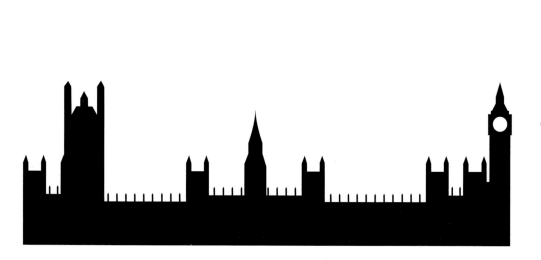
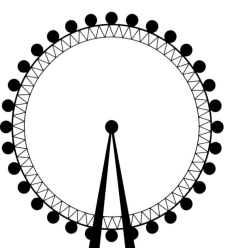

Contents

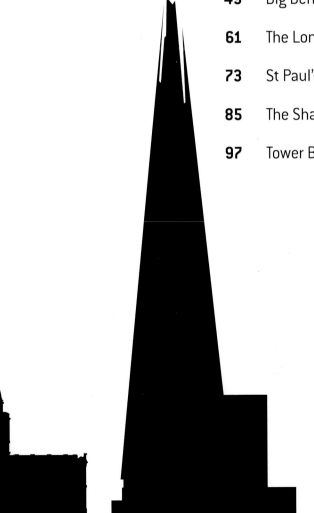

Introduction

No other city on Earth is quite like London. Standing on the River Thames in the south-eastern corner of the United Kingdom, the world's most visited city is a melting pot of history and culture. Its history stretches back more than two millennia to Roman times and – it is thought – even earlier still. Today, it is a fascinating place of contrasts, where ages-old tradition meets modernity and unexpected reminders of the significant role it has played on the world stage can be found around every corner.

The London story is one of almost continual growth. Now a global leader in the arts, finance, fashion and entertainment, during its long history the city has been a battleground, the seat of kings and queens, a political hotbed and force for global change, the heart of history's largest empire and an economic powerhouse. It has witnessed plagues, devastating fires and bombs, as well as national celebrations and important international events, such as the Great Exhibition of 1851. It is the city of Elizabeth I, William Shakespeare, Jack the Ripper, the Bloomsbury Set, the Swinging Sixties and the Olympic Games, which it has hosted three times – the only city to have done so. London's museums and art galleries house some of the greatest collections in the world. There are iconic symbols of the city at every turn, from its familiar red telephone boxes, double-decker buses and black cabs to its soaring structures.

Indeed, London's jumble of architectural styles plays a key role in shaping its distinctive character. In few other cities can you find Georgian houses, hypermodern offices and unexpected delights such as Tudor pubs rubbing shoulders in quite such close proximity. It is not an overstatement to say that London has some of the best-known works of architecture in the world – the Tower of London, Buckingham Palace and Trafalgar Square, to name a few – as well as a remarkable number of parks, gardens and green spaces. Within its 32 boroughs are buildings ranging from Roman ruins to 21st-century marvels such as the glittering Shard tower, and everything in between.

Celebrating London's buildings, this book is as unique as the city itself. There are any number of books covering the history of London and its architecture, but this one offers something a little different – the chance to get up close to those buildings by making your own models. The five buildings included are among the best-known of London's many famous sights: Sir Christopher Wren's masterpiece St Paul's Cathedral, the Houses of Parliament with its world-famous "Big Ben" clock tower, Tower Bridge, the London Eye and the Shard. Each is accompanied by facts and figures that give some background information to bring your very own miniature London alive.

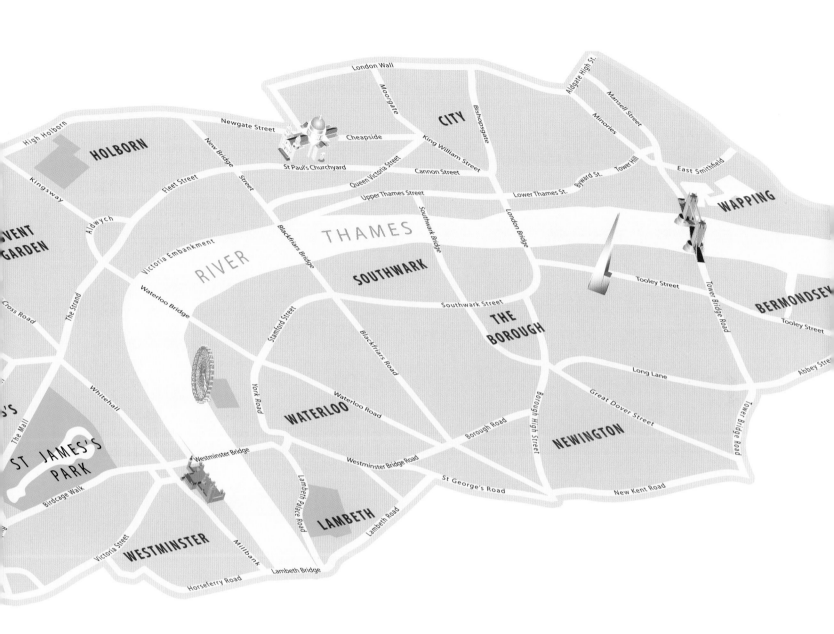

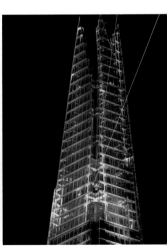

Big Ben and the Houses of Parliament

QUICK FACTS

Architects: Sir Charles Barry; Augustus Pugin
Designed: 1835
Completed: 1870
Height: 323 feet (98.5 m) Victoria Tower;
316 feet (96 m) Elizabeth Tower;
299 feet (91 m) Central Tower
Size: 8 acres (3.24 hectares)
A UNESCO World Heritage Site

In a city full of iconic landmarks, no building is quite so universally famous as Big Ben and the Houses of Parliament. Printed onto countless postcards and often used as visual shorthand by filmmakers who want their audience to immediately identify the setting, they say "London" in the same way that the Empire State Building says "New York" or the Eiffel Tower says "Paris". It is slightly odd, then, that neither is commonly known by its proper name. "Big Ben" is actually the name of the largest bell housed in what was originally known simply as the "Clock Tower", renamed "Elizabeth Tower" in 2012 to commemorate the Diamond Jubilee of Queen Elizabeth II. The building we know as the Houses of Parliament is officially called the Palace of Westminster. It's more common to call them Big Ben or the Houses of Parliament, although both names refer to the same building.

A principal royal residence since the 11th century, the original palace caught fire in 1834 and large parts of it were destroyed. The following year, a Royal Commission announced a competition to design a replacement, with a prize of £1,500. From 96 submissions, they chose a Gothic-inspired structure designed on Classical principles of symmetry by Charles Barry, while interior decoration – as well as the Elizabeth Tower – was added by Augustus Pugin, a champion of the Neo-Gothic style. Barry's plan incorporated surviving parts of the first palace, notably the vast Westminster Hall, which dates to 1097.

Both architects died before the palace was finished, but the result of their work is an elaborately detailed masterpiece and a suitably imposing seat for the British government, "bookended" by the Victoria Tower on its south-western corner and by the Elizabeth Tower at the northern end. The clock itself has been reliably marking time to within a second of the hour since its installation in 1859 and chimes on the quarter hour with four smaller bells and on the hour with Big Ben (or the Great Bell of Westminster, to give it its official name). The 13.8 tonne bell's distinctive sound is due to a crack that appeared after it was hung. In the middle of the complex is the octagonal Central Tower, which rises over the Central Lobby (originally the Octagon Hall). This was described by

Above: An aerial view of Big Ben and the Houses of Parliament.

Opposite: Big Ben lit up at night. The Great Bell's strikes were heard for the first time on 11 July 1859 and the quarter bells on 7 September that year.

Erskine May, a 19th-century expert on the British constitution, as "the political centre of the British Empire" because of its position between the Lords and Commons chambers. When standing beneath the chandelier of the Central Lobby, it is possible to see both the Speaker's Chair in the Commons Chamber and the Royal Throne in the Lords Chamber – as long as the doors are open, of course.

Sumptuously decorated with vaulted ceilings, carved stonework and stained glass windows, the Palace of Westminster contains more than 1,100 rooms – including offices for MPs, lobbies, restaurants and bars, libraries and state apartments for the Speaker of the House and the Lord Chancellor. The complex also has a number of courtyards, small gardens and a terrace overlooking the river.

Above: Big Ben and the Houses of Parliament, seen from across the River Thames.

Opposite, above: Created by Baron Carlo Marochetti and completed in 1856, the statue of King Richard I is located in Old Palace Yard outside the Houses of Parliament.

Opposite, below: St Stephen's Porch, the public entrance to the Houses of Parliament. Once you pass through the doors and enter the Central Lobby, the Commons Chamber is to the left and the Lords Chamber to the right.

Instructions

⚙ This symbol means that you should fold the pieces indicated along the indented fold lines before connecting the tabs and slots.

Step 1

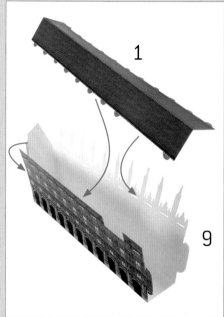

⚙ 1, 9

Push all the Q and R tabs on piece 1 into the corresponding Q and R slots on piece 9, from inside to outside.
Fold tabs A1 and B1 on piece 9.
Push tab A on piece 9 into slot A1 on piece 9.
Push tab B on piece 9 into slot B1 on piece 9.

Step 2

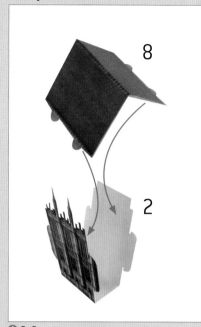

⚙ 2, 8

Push tabs BB and CC on piece 8 into the corresponding slots on piece 2, from inside to outside.

Step 3

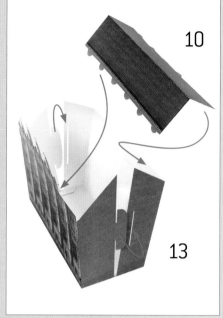

⚙ 10, 13

Push the PP and QQ tabs on piece 10 into the corresponding slots on piece 13, from inside to outside.
Push tabs NN and TT on piece 13 into the corresponding slots on piece 13.

Step 4

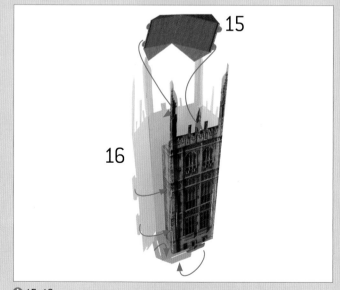

⚙ 15, 16

Fold the T1 tabs on piece 16.
Push the V and W tabs on piece 15 into the corresponding slots on piece 16, from inside to outside.
Starting with the base and working upwards, push the T tabs on piece 16 into the T1 slots on piece 16.
Fold tab U1 on piece 16.
Push tab U on piece 16 into slot U1 on piece 16. .

Step 5

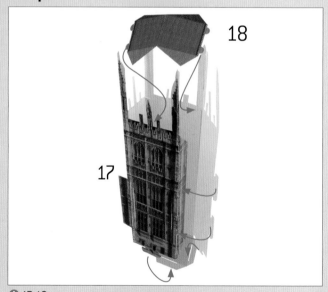

⚙ 17, 18

Fold the X1 tabs on piece 17.
Push the AA and Z tabs on piece 18 into the corresponding slots on piece 17, from inside to outside.
Starting with the base and working upwards, push the X tabs on piece 17 into the X1 slots on piece 17.
Fold tab Y1 on piece 17.
Push tab Y on piece 17 into slot Y1 on piece 17.

Step 6

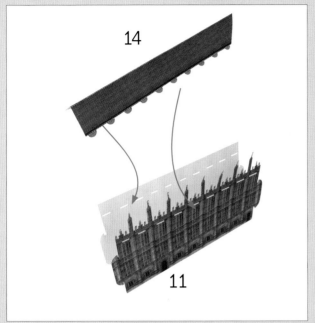

⚠ 11, 14
Push the HH and II tabs on piece 14 into the corresponding slots on piece 11, from inside to outside.

Step 7

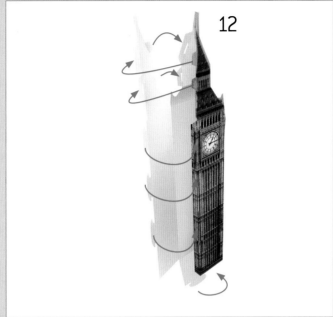

⚠ 12
Fold the C1 tabs.
Starting with the base and working upwards, push the C tabs on piece 12 into the C1 slots on piece 12.
Fold all the tabs on the spires of piece 12.
Push the tabs on the spires of piece 12 into the slots on the spires of piece 12 (i.e. L1 into L1, L2 into L2, etc.).
Fold the P1 tabs. Push tab P into the corresponding slot P1.

Step 8

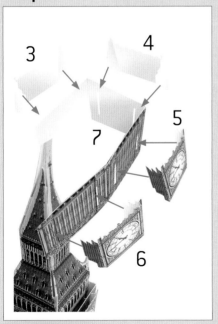

⚠ 3, 4, 5, 6, 7
Push the tabs on pieces 3, 4, 5 and 6 into the corresponding slots on piece 7 (i.e. D into D1, E into E1, etc.). Make sure that they are pushed all the way through.

Step 9

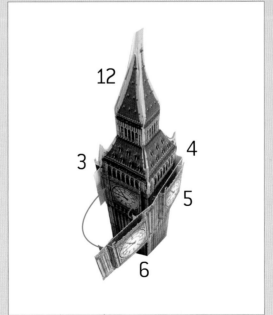

Push the tabs on pieces 3, 4, 5 and 6 that are now pushed though piece 7 into the corresponding slots on piece 12 (i.e. D into D2, E into E2, etc.).

Step 10

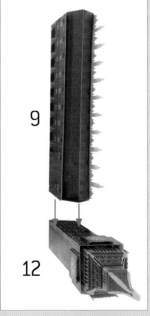

Push the S tabs on piece 9 into the S slots on piece 12.

Step 11

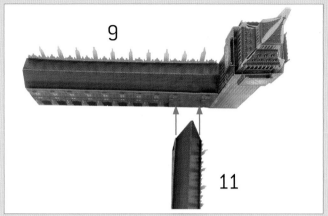

Push tabs JJ and KK on piece 11 into the corresponding slots on piece 9.

Step 12

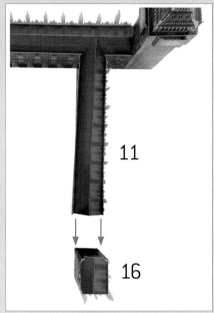

Push tabs MM and LL on piece 11 into the corresponding slots on piece 16.

Step 13

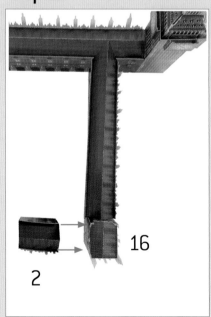

Push tabs DD and EE on piece 2 into the corresponding slots on piece 16.

Step 14

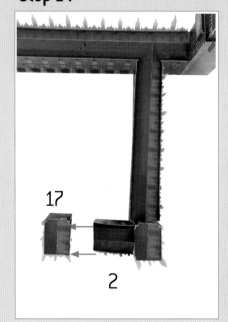

Push tabs FF and GG on piece 2 into the corresponding slots on piece 17.

Step 15

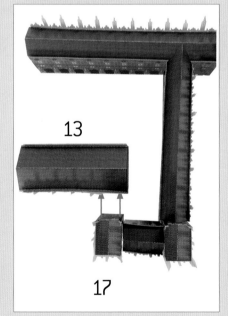

Push tabs RR and SS on piece 17 into the corresponding slots on piece 13.

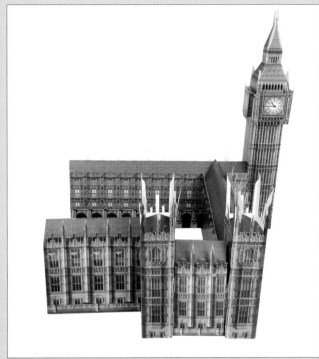

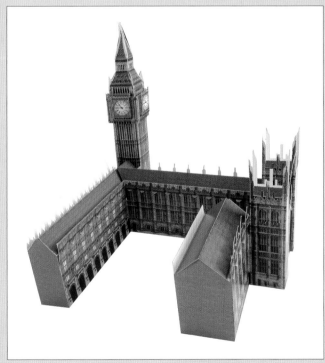

The London Eye

QUICK FACTS

Name: Originally known as the British Airways London Eye; due to changes of ownership and sponsorship deals, its official name is currently the EDF Energy London Eye.

Constructed: 1998–1999

Architects: Frank Anatole, Nic Bailey, Steve Chilton, Malcolm Cook, Mark Sparrowhawk, Julia Barfield and David Marks.

Height: 443 feet (135 m)

Wheel diameter: 394 feet (120 m)

Weight: 2,100 tonnes

Below: The London Eye at night.

With its spectacular views over London and elegant design, the London Eye has become one of the city's most admired landmarks. Sometimes called the "Millennium Wheel", the giant Ferris wheel was opened by Prime Minister Tony Blair on 31 December 1999 – the final day of the second millennium – although due to teething problems it did not begin transporting visitors into the London skies until the following March. Since then, the London Eye has drawn in 3.5 million visitors every year, making it the most popular tourist attraction in Britain.

The construction of this British icon has, in fact, become a symbol of European cooperation. The steel,

although British, was engineered in the Netherlands, the cables were made in Italy and the capsules in France, with other parts coming from the Czech Republic and Germany. Each of the wheel's sixteen sections was floated up the Thames on a barge and joined to its neighbour on pontoons in the river before being slowly winched into place by specialist cranes. Each of its 32 capsules, representing the 32 boroughs of London, seats 25 people, meaning up to 800 passengers can be carried at the same time – about the same as 11 double-decker buses.

The enormous observation wheel is not, in fact, London's first. In 1895, the Earls Court Empire of India Exhibition unveiled the "Great Wheel", which had a diameter of 270 feet (82.3 m). Situated on the South Bank of the Thames, across the river from Big Ben and the Houses of Parliament, the Great Wheel's larger descendant was the world's biggest Ferris wheel until the construction of the Star of Nanchang in China in 2006 (itself topped by the Singapore Flyer in 2008). The highest point of the London Eye stands at 443 feet (135 m), and the wheel itself has a diameter of 394 feet (120 m). The vast rim of the wheel is supported by tensioned steel cables and rotates at 10 inches (26 cm) per second (0.6 mph, or 0.9 kph) – a speed that means each revolution takes about half an hour and allows able-bodied visitors to walk on and off

without stopping the wheel. Electrical motors turn the observation capsules to keep the floor level during the ride.

Designed by a consortium of architects, the Eye has earned praise from many quarters, including Richard Rogers, who has likened its impact on the London skyline to that of the Eiffel Tower on Paris. For those who take a ride in one of its air-conditioned capsules, it offers incredible vistas of up to 25 miles (40 km) over one of the world's greatest cities – weather permitting!

Left: A side-on view of the London Eye from Westminster Bridge.

Below: The view from one of the pods on the London Eye. Big Ben and the Houses of Parliament can be seen on the right of the picture.

Opposite: The London Eye seen from across the River Thames.

Instructions

⚠ This symbol means that you should fold the pieces indicated along the indented fold lines before connecting the tabs and slots.

Step 1

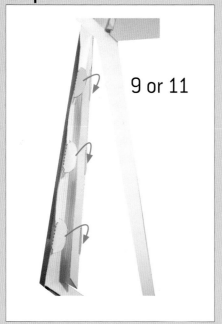

9 or 11

⚠ 9, 11
Push the A tabs on piece 9 into the A slots on piece 9.
Push the B tabs on piece 11 into the B tabs on piece 11.

Step 2

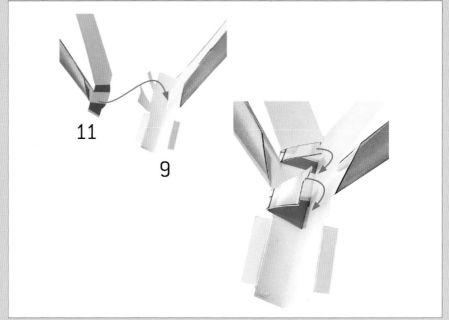

11

9

Push tab C on piece 11 into slot C on piece 9 (NB: tab C should push through from the underside, so that the artwork on both pieces 9 and 11 is facing outwards).
Fold the V tabs on piece 9 down flat to the blue shaded areas on piece 11.

Step 3

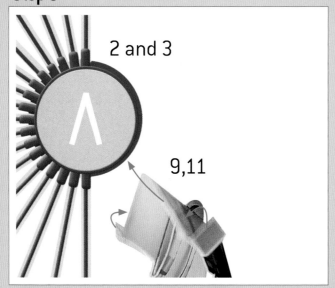

2 and 3

9,11

Fold the E and D tabs on piece 9 back on themselves and push them through the v-shaped slot in piece 2 (NB: the numbered and shaded central circle on piece 2 should be facing away from pieces 9 and 11).
Repeat this process with piece 3 (again with the numbered and shaded central circle facing away from pieces 9 and 11).
Fold down the E tabs to lock pieces 2 and 3 in place.

Step 4

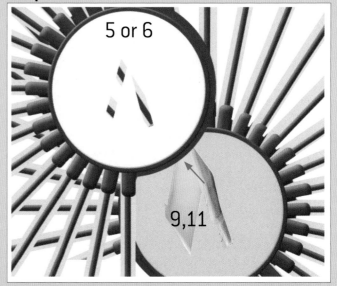

5 or 6

9,11

Keep the D tabs on piece 9 folded flat and push them through the v-shaped slot on piece 5 (NB: the numbered and shaded central circle on piece 5 should be facing towards pieces 9 and 11).
Repeat this process with piece 6 (again with the numbered and shaded central circle facing towards pieces 9 and 11).
Now fold out the D tabs on piece 9 to secure pieces 4 and 5 in position.

Step 5

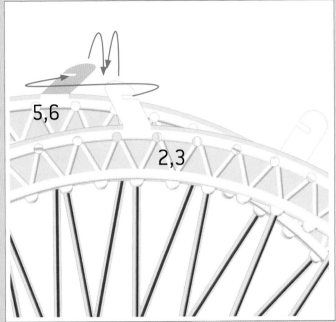

5,6

2,3

Clip all the F tabs on pieces 2 and 3 into all of the G tabs on pieces 5 and 6.

Step 6

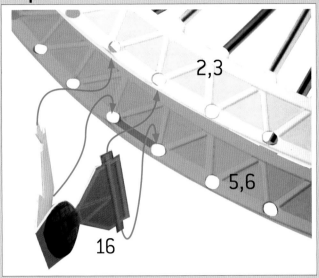

2,3

5,6

16

⌃ 16, all the 1s
Push the tabs on piece 16 into the slots at the bottom of the wheel (NB: the appropriate slots are marked with a blue line between them on both sides of the inside of the wheel).
All the remaining pods are numbered as 1. Push these into the wheel, one tab per slot, in a clockwise or anticlockwise direction from next to where the bottom pod (piece 2) was placed.

Step 7

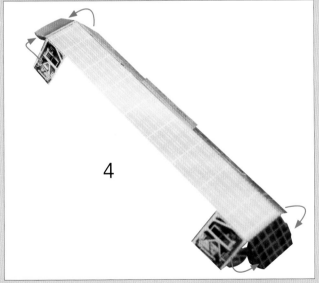

4

⌃ 4
Push the H tabs on piece 4 into the H slots on piece 4.
Push the H1 tabs on piece 4 into the H1 slots on piece 4.

Step 8

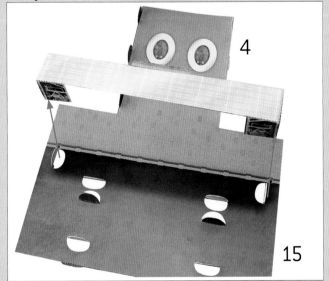

4

15

Fold tab J on piece 15 and push it into slot J on piece 4.
Fold tab K on piece 15 and push it into slot K on piece 4

Step 9

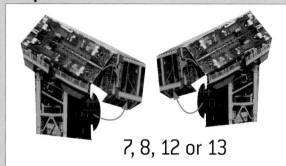

7, 8, 12 or 13

⚠ 7, 8, 12, 13
Piece 7: Fold tab M flat. Push tab L into slot L. NB: tab M should sit inside the piece, as shown in the diagram.
Piece 8: Fold tab O flat. Push tab N into slot N. NB: tab O should sit inside the piece, as shown in the diagram.
Piece 12: Fold tab Q flat. Push tab P into slot P. NB: tab Q should sit inside the piece, as shown in the diagram.
Piece 13: Fold tab S flat. Push tab R into slot R. NB: tab S should sit inside the piece, as shown in the diagram.

Step 10

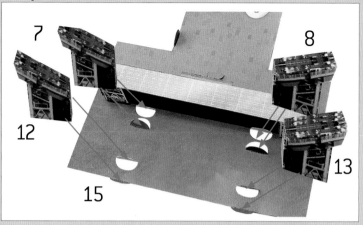

Fold tabs T and T1 on piece 15 and push them into the corresponding slots on piece 7.
Fold tabs U and U1 on piece 15 and push them into the corresponding slots on piece 8.
Fold tabs V and V1 on piece 15 and push them into the corresponding slots on piece 12.
Fold tabs W and W1 on piece 15 and push them into the corresponding slots on piece 13.

Step 11

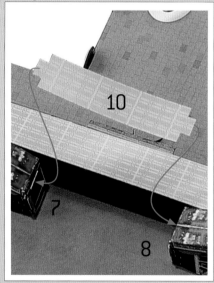

Push tabs X and X1 on piece 10 into the corresponding slots on pieces 7 and 8.

Step 12

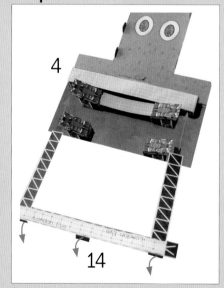

Push tabs Y and Y1 on piece 14 into slots Y and Y1 on piece 4.
Fold the Z tabs on piece 14 to 90 degrees to hold this piece up.

Step 13

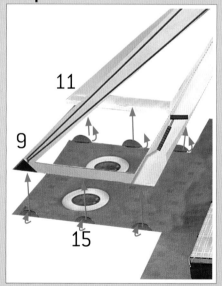

Fold the AA tabs on piece 15 and push them into the AA slots on piece 9.
Fold the BB tabs on piece 15 and push them into the BB slots on piece 11.
Fold the CC tab on piece 15 and push it into the CC slot on the bottom of piece 2 (the bottom pod on the wheel).

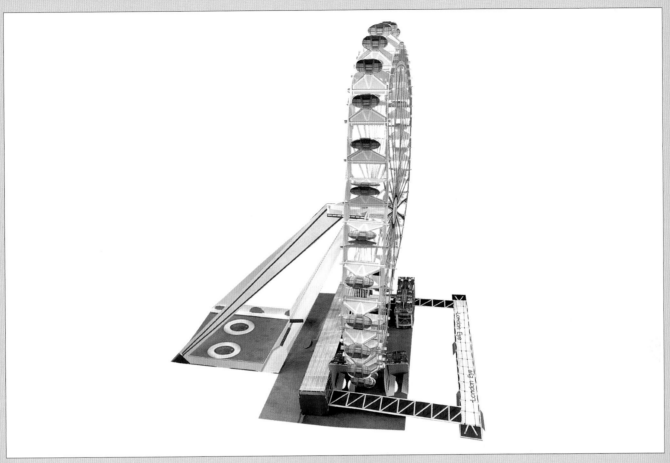

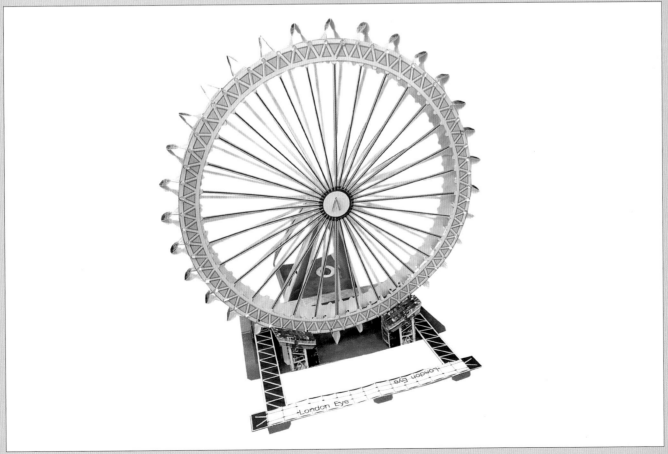

St Paul's Cathedral

QUICK FACTS

Name: St Paul's Cathedral
Architect: Sir Christopher Wren
Designed: 1668–1675
Completed: 1711
Height: 365 feet (111 m)
Length: 518 feet (158 m)
Width (across transepts): 246 feet (75 m)

Standing on Ludgate Hill, at the highest point in the City of London, St Paul's Cathedral has dominated the skyline for over three centuries and is undoubtedly among the world's most famous buildings. Until 1962 it was the tallest building in the city and today remains a cherished part of the nation's heritage. Since its consecration on 2 December 1697, it has hosted some of Britain's most momentous events — including the funerals of the great Duke of Wellington and Sir Winston Churchill, jubilee celebrations of Queen Victoria and Queen Elizabeth II, and the marriage of Prince Charles to Lady Diana Spencer — as well as becoming a symbol of the indomitable British spirit during the Nazi bombing of World War II, which it survived almost unscathed. In fact, the present St Paul's is the fifth to have stood on the site. The first was founded over 1,400 years ago in 604, and while its fate remains a mystery, it is known that at least three were subsequently destroyed by fire (medieval London, with its wood and thatch houses, was particularly prone). The present cathedral's predecessor burned down during the Great Fire of London in 1666.

The task of designing a replacement was awarded to Sir Christopher Wren in 1668. A renowned scientist working during an age when today's boundaries between scientific disciplines and related professions did not exist, Wren designed no fewer than 52 of London's churches (as well as numerous other buildings), although St Paul's is unquestionably his masterpiece. In fact, Wren had been involved in renovating the rather dilapidated cathedral for several years before it was gutted by fire and had already designed a dome to replace its tower. After the fire, the decision was taken to replace the ruined structure with a new, modern building, and over the following years Wren produced a series of designs, each more ambitious than the last.

Construction started in 1675 and was declared completed in 1711, although some detail remained to be added. The finished cathedral is a superb expression of Baroque design, built with Classical symmetry and infused with influences from English medieval church architecture. Like many cathedrals, it is built to a cruciform plan, with transepts jutting

from the main body. The focal point of the exterior is the magnificent, graceful dome, which soars above the city to a height of 365 feet (111 m) at the top of its crowning spire and remains one of the world's highest. Inside, the cathedral is richly ornamented with sculpture, paintings and mosaics by some of the country's greatest artists and craftsmen. Beneath this breathtaking grandeur are extensive crypts and tombs where some of the most famous of Britain's historical figures are interred – among them Admiral Lord Nelson, Florence Nightingale and Samuel Johnson. The first person to be laid to rest within St Paul's Cathedral was, fittingly, Sir Christopher Wren himself, in 1723.

Above: An aerial view of St Paul's Cathedral and the surrounding area.

Opposite: The dome of St Paul's Cathedral; Wren drew inspiration for its design from Michelangelo's dome of St Peter's Basilica in the Vatican City and that of Mansart's Church of the Val-de-Grâce in Paris.

Above: A view of St Paul's Cathedral from across the surrounding gardens.

Opposite, above: The clock in the south-west tower, built in 1893, is the most recent of the clocks added to the cathedral over the centuries.

Opposite, below: The west front of St Paul's Cathedral, featuring Francis Bird's statue of Queen Anne, who was reigning monarch at the time of the cathedral's completion.

Instructions

⚠ This symbol means that you should fold the pieces indicated along the indented fold lines before connecting the tabs and slots.

Step 1

⚠ 12

Push tabs A, B, C and D on piece 12 into the corresponding slots on piece 12.

Step 2

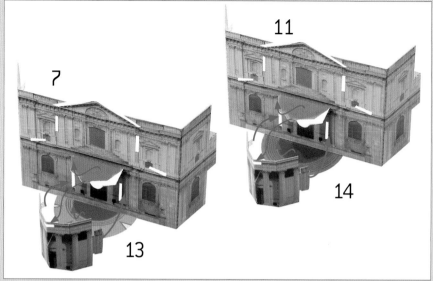

⚠ 7, 11, 13, 14

Fold M and M1 on piece 7 so that they sit at a 90-degree angle to the building.

Fold tabs N and N1 on piece 13 back on themselves and push them into the corresponding slots on piece 7.

Push tab M1 on piece 7 into slot M1 on piece 13.

Fold E and E1 on piece 11.

Fold tabs F and F1 on piece 14 back on themselves and push them into the corresponding slots on piece 11.

Push tab E1 on piece 11 into slot E1 on piece 14.

Step 3

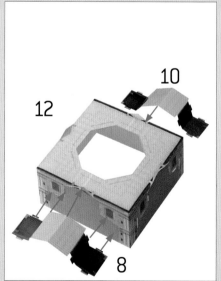

⚠ 8, 10

Push the O and P tabs on piece 8 and the G and H tabs on piece 10 into the corresponding slots in piece 12.

Push the sloped roofs on pieces 8 and 10 into place in the v-shaped slots on piece 12.

Step 4

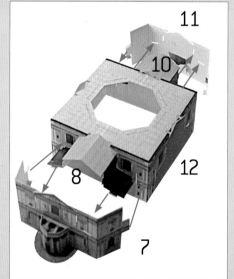

Push the S and T tabs on piece 7 and the L and K tabs on piece 11 into the corresponding slots on piece 12.

Push the Q and R tabs on piece 8 and the J and I tabs on piece 10 into the corresponding slots on pieces 7 and 11.

Step 5

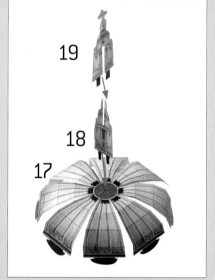

Push the tabs on piece 18 into the slots on piece 17 (any combination of tabs into slots is fine).

Push piece 19 into piece 18.

Push the tabs on piece 19 into the slots on piece 17.

Step 6

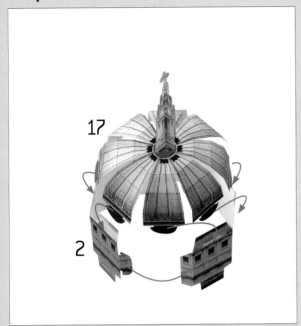

⌂ 2, 17

Push the YY tabs on piece 17 into the YY slots on piece 2 (any combination of tabs into slots is fine).

Push tab XX on piece 2 into slot XX in piece 2.

Step 7

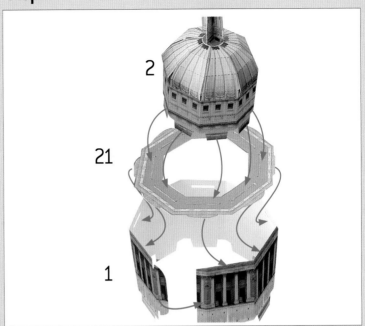

⌂ 1

Push the WW tabs on piece 2 into the WW slots on piece 21 (any combination of tabs into slots is fine).

Push tab UU on piece 1 into slot UU on piece 1.

Push the TT tabs on piece 21 into the TT slots on piece 1 (any combination of tabs into slots is fine).

Step 8

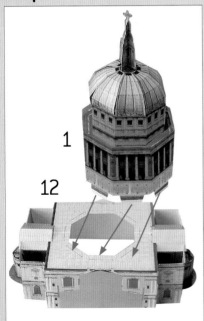

Push the VV tabs on piece 1 into the VV slots on piece 12 (any combination of tabs into slots is fine).

Step 9

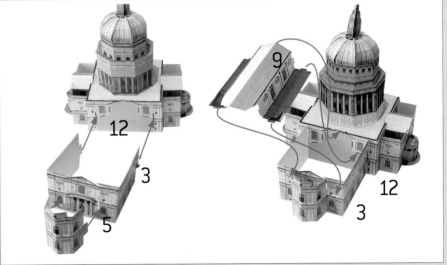

⌂ 3, 9

Fold tabs Y and Z on piece 5 back on themselves and push them into the corresponding slots on piece 3.

Fold tabs AA and BB on piece 3 back on themselves and push them into the corresponding slots on piece 12.

Push the sloped roof on piece 9 into place in the v-shaped slots on piece 12.

Push the U and V tabs on piece 9 into the corresponding slots on piece 12.

Push the W and X tabs on piece 9 into the corresponding slots on piece 3.

Step 10

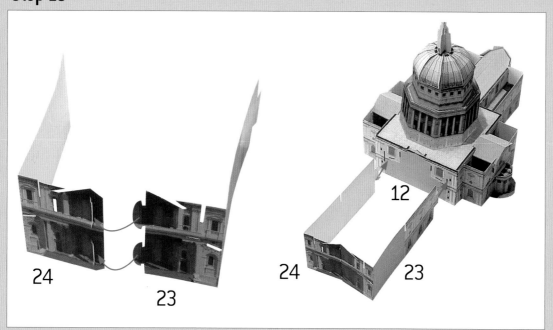

⊗ 23, 24

Push the CC tabs on piece 23 into the corresponding slots on piece 24.

Fold the II tab on piece 23 and the HH tab on piece 24 back on themselves and push them into the corresponding slots on piece 12.

Step 11

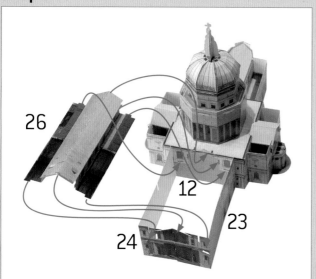

⊗ 26

Push the sloped roof on piece 26 into place in the v-shaped slots on piece 12.

Push the DD and EE tabs on piece 26 into the corresponding slots on piece 12.

Push the sloped roof on piece 26 into place in the v-shaped slots on pieces 23 and 24.

Push the FF and GG tabs on piece 26 into the corresponding slots on pieces 23 and 24.

Step 12

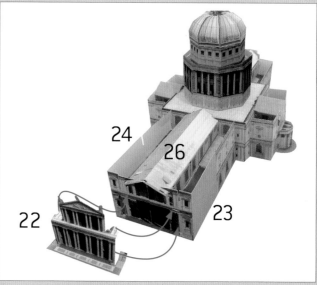

⊗ 22

Press piece 26 (the roof) slightly flat. Push the statues on the top of piece 22 into the slots in piece 26.

Push the JJ tabs on piece 22 into the corresponding slots on pieces 23 and 24.

Press the OO tabs on piece 22 flat up against pieces 23 and 24. These will be held in place by pieces 4 and 6 when they are added in step 14.

Step 13

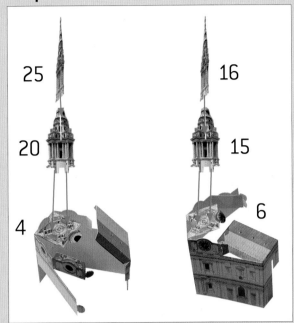

⌃ 4, 6

Push the KK tabs on piece 20 into the KK slots on piece 4 (any combination of tabs into slots is fine). Push piece 25 into piece 20. Push the KK tabs on piece 25 into the KK slots on piece 4. Push the PP tabs on piece 15 into the PP slots on piece 6 (any combination of tabs into slots is fine). Push piece 16 into piece 15. Push the PP tabs on piece 16 into the PP slots on piece 6.

Step 14

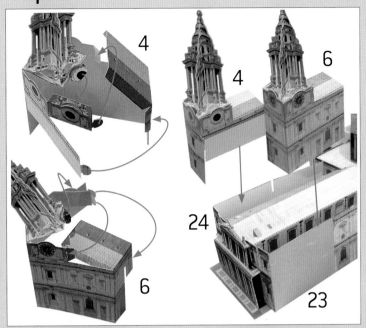

On piece 4: Push tab LL into slot LL, tab MM into slot MM, and tab NN into slot NN.

Slot piece 4 onto the side of piece 24, making sure that tab OO on piece 22 is held behind piece 4 as it drops down.

On piece 6: Push tab QQ into slot QQ, tab RR into slot RR, and tab SS into slot SS.

Slot piece 6 onto the side of piece 23, making sure that tab OO on piece 22 is held behind piece 6 as it drops down.

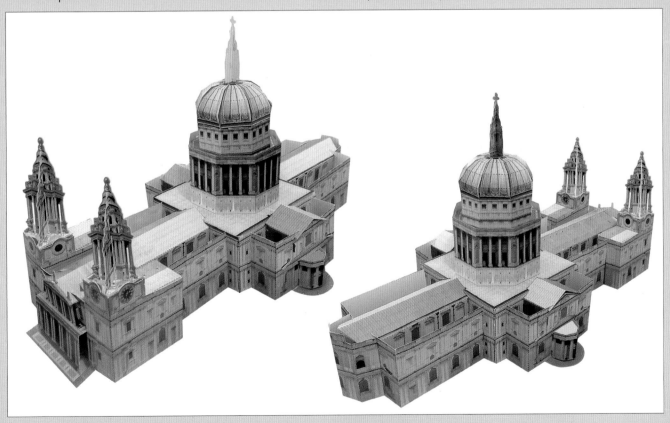

The Shard

QUICK FACTS

Name: The Shard
Architect: Renzo Piano
Designed: 2000
Completed: 2012
Height: 1,016 feet (309.6 m)
Floor space: 27 acres (11 hectares)

Below: The Shard, pictured at sunset with London's new City Hall building (completed 2002) visible on the far left of the picture.

Opposite: A view looking up the side of the Shard at some of the 11,000 panes of glass that make up its exterior.

Standing 1,016 feet (309.6 m) high, the Shard dwarfs its closest rival in the city – One Canada Square – by more than 230 feet (70 m) and is the tallest building in the European Union. Opened in July 2012 to great fanfare amidst a fantastic light show with lasers reflecting from its glass cladding, the shining spire has attracted equal amounts of both criticism and praise. Indeed, somewhat ironically, it owes its name to detractors at English Heritage, an organization committed to preserving the country's historic landscape, who said the building would "tear through historic London like a shard of glass". Originally called "London Bridge Tower" due to its proximity to the older landmark, the structure is now universally known as the Shard.

Designed by the acclaimed Italian architect Renzo Piano, the building was conceived in 2000, when entrepreneur Irvine Sellar and Piano met for lunch to discuss the possible development of Southwark Towers, a characterless office block that stood on the site. It is reported that after pouring scorn

on conventional skyscrapers, Piano immediately sketched an idea for a simple and elegant spire on the back of the restaurant's menu. His inspirations were the masts of tall sailing ships on the Thames and the London church spires depicted in antique etchings and paintings of the city. Building consent was not awarded until 2003, due to fierce opposition from conservation groups, and further delays were caused by securing the £350 million funding (later raised to £435 million) and the careful demolition of Southwark Towers.

In March 2009, however, work finally began and the tower's 500 tonne, 217 foot (66 m) crowning spire was fixed in place three years later. The final panes of glass (the building has 11,000) were fitted shortly after. The finished building is largely made from recycled materials and is an undeniably stylish addition to the London skyline. In the architect's words, it is a "vertical city". Inside, it contains 72

occupiable floors, with the lowest given over to retail and office space, featuring winter gardens made possible by the building's careful design on every floor. Floors 31 to 33 offer restaurants and bars with fabulous views over the city, while the sumptuous five-star Shangri-La Hotel can be found on floors 34 to 52. Above the hotel are 13 floors of private residences, with luxury apartments in the building fetching upwards of £30 million, and the highest floors are observation decks that offer magnificent 360-degree views of the city and beyond from 804 feet (244 m) – almost double the height of the London Eye. From there, visitors can see at least 40 miles (64 km) and some claim that it's even possible to spot France on a clear day.

Right and opposite, below: The Shard pictured during the light and laser show on its opening in July 2012.

Opposite, above: The Shard, piercing the sky and dwarfing the surrounding buildings.

Instructions

⌃ This symbol means that you should fold the pieces indicated along the indented fold lines before connecting the tabs and slots.

Step 1

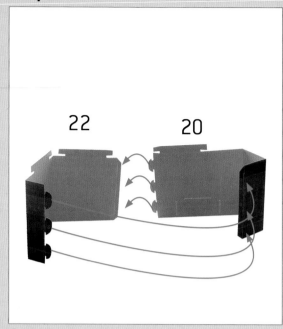

⌃ 20, 22

Fold the F tabs on piece 20. Fold the E tabs on piece 22. Push the F tabs on piece 20 into the F slots on piece 22. Push the E tabs on piece 22 into the E slots on piece 20.

Step 2

⌃ 21

Push the G tabs on piece 21 into the G slots on piece 22. Push the H tabs on piece 21 into the H slots on piece 20.

Step 3

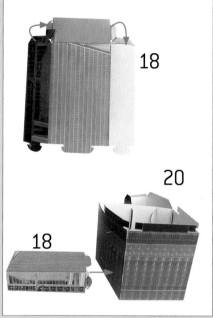

⌃ 18

Push the I tabs on piece 18 into the I slots on piece 18. Push the J tabs on piece 18 into the J slots on piece 20.

Step 4

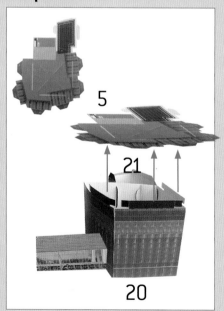

Fold tab K1 on piece 20 and tabs K2 and K3 on piece 22 back on themselves and push them into the corresponding slots on piece 5. Push the L tabs on piece 5 into the corresponding slots on piece 21.

Step 5

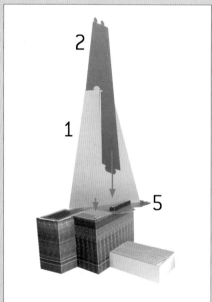

Push tabs A and A1 on piece 1 into the corresponding slots on piece 5. Slot piece 2 into piece 1, then push tabs B and B1 on piece 2 into the corresponding slots in piece 5.

Step 6

⌃ 19

Push tabs C, C1, D and D1 on pieces 1 and 2 through the corresponding slots on piece 19.

Step 7

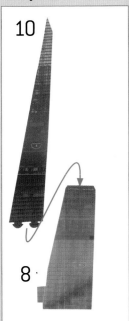

10

8

Step 8

13

14

Step 9

11

12

Step 10

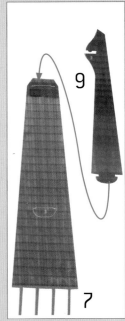

6

15

Step 11

6

9

7

⚠ 8
Push tabs M and M1 on piece 10 through the corresponding slots on piece 8.

Push tabs N and N1 on piece 13 through the corresponding slots on piece 14.

Push tabs X and X1 on piece 11 through the corresponding slots on piece 12.

Push tab CC on piece 6 through slot CC on piece 15.

Push tab FF on piece 9 through slot FF on piece 7.

Step 12

4

3

Step 13

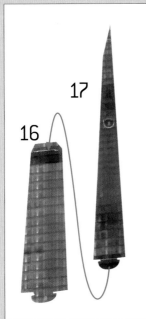

17

16

Step 14

24

23

Push tab ll on piece 4 through slot ll on piece 3.

Push tab LL on piece 17 through slot LL on piece 16.

Push tabs P and P1 on piece 24 through the corresponding slots on piece 23.

Step 15

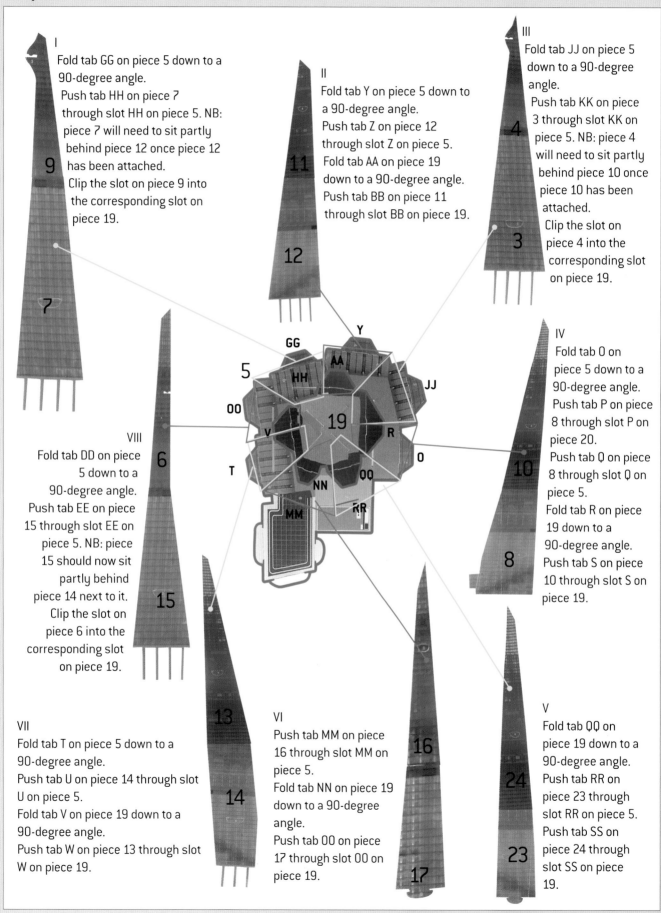

I
Fold tab GG on piece 5 down to a 90-degree angle.
Push tab HH on piece 7 through slot HH on piece 5. NB: piece 7 will need to sit partly behind piece 12 once piece 12 has been attached.
Clip the slot on piece 9 into the corresponding slot on piece 19.

II
Fold tab Y on piece 5 down to a 90-degree angle.
Push tab Z on piece 12 through slot Z on piece 5.
Fold tab AA on piece 19 down to a 90-degree angle.
Push tab BB on piece 11 through slot BB on piece 19.

III
Fold tab JJ on piece 5 down to a 90-degree angle.
Push tab KK on piece 3 through slot KK on piece 5. NB: piece 4 will need to sit partly behind piece 10 once piece 10 has been attached.
Clip the slot on piece 4 into the corresponding slot on piece 19.

IV
Fold tab O on piece 5 down to a 90-degree angle.
Push tab P on piece 8 through slot P on piece 20.
Push tab Q on piece 8 through slot Q on piece 5.
Fold tab R on piece 19 down to a 90-degree angle.
Push tab S on piece 10 through slot S on piece 19.

V
Fold tab QQ on piece 19 down to a 90-degree angle.
Push tab RR on piece 23 through slot RR on piece 5.
Push tab SS on piece 24 through slot SS on piece 19.

VI
Push tab MM on piece 16 through slot MM on piece 5.
Fold tab NN on piece 19 down to a 90-degree angle.
Push tab OO on piece 17 through slot OO on piece 19.

VII
Fold tab T on piece 5 down to a 90-degree angle.
Push tab U on piece 14 through slot U on piece 5.
Fold tab V on piece 19 down to a 90-degree angle.
Push tab W on piece 13 through slot W on piece 19.

VIII
Fold tab DD on piece 5 down to a 90-degree angle.
Push tab EE on piece 15 through slot EE on piece 5. NB: piece 15 should now sit partly behind piece 14 next to it.
Clip the slot on piece 6 into the corresponding slot on piece 19.

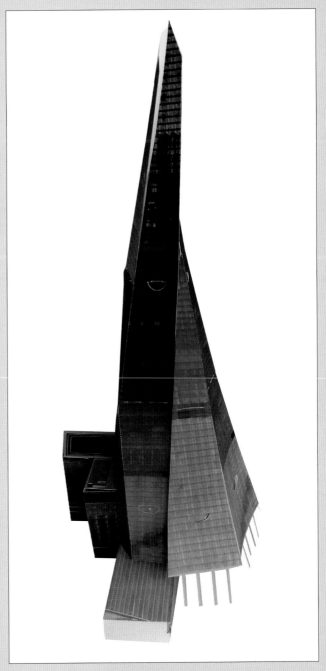

Tower Bridge

QUICK FACTS

Name: Tower Bridge
Architects: Sir Horace Jones; George D. Stevenson (who replaced Jones when he died in 1887)
Designed: 1884
Completed: 1894
Tower height: 213 feet (65 m)
Size: 8 acres (3.24 hectares)
Total length: 801 feet (244 m)
Central span: 200 feet (61 m)

Below: A panoramic view of Tower Bridge.

Opposite: A view along one of the pedestrian walkways of Tower Bridge at night.

Spanning the Thames and connecting the boroughs of Tower Hamlets and Southwark, Tower Bridge was the largest and most sophisticated combined bascule and suspension bridge in the world at the time of its construction. Providing an imposing gateway into the heart of London for river traffic, it is now – like Big Ben and St Paul's Cathedral – one of the city's most iconic structures.

The bridge's history dates back to the late nineteenth century. Victorian London was expanding rapidly and, while new bridges had been built to the west of London Bridge (the city's oldest), the area to the east had become much more densely populated. For anyone who lived there, a river crossing meant a frustrating journey through busy streets to London Bridge. A new thoroughfare across the river was desperately needed. Nevertheless, bridging the Thames was no simple proposition as the area was also economically dependent on the tall-masted ships sailing up-river to dock at the Pool of London. In 1876, the City of London Corporation threw the problem open to competition, inviting submissions for a bridge design that would allow both pedestrians and vehicles to cross the river while not impeding vessels beneath.

More than 50 proposals were received, but it wasn't until 1884 that the design of City Architect Sir Horace Jones (who also happened to sit on the judging panel of the Special Bridge or Subway Committee) was

finally approved. Aided by the engineer Sir John Wolfe Barry, Jones proposed a bridge with a central span composed of two bascules (the word "bascule" derives from the French for "see-saw"), bracketed by towers, with short suspension bridges to either side. With towers designed specifically to complement those of the nearby Tower of London (from which the bridge takes its name) housing the hydraulic machinery, the bascules could be raised as necessary, allowing ships to pass, while a walkway 143 feet (44 m) above the river would allow pedestrians to cross whether they were raised or lowered.

Work began in 1886, with foundations for the towers being sunk into the Thames riverbed. For the next eight years, 432 men worked to make Jones's design a reality. Officially opened on 30 June 1894 by the Prince of Wales (later King Edward VII) and his wife, the finished bridge is 801 feet (244 m) in length with a central span of 200 feet (61 m). For well over

a century, it has served its purpose admirably and, while its distinctive, Gothic-style towers were much criticized when the bridge was completed, they have since become a much-loved emblem of the city. Although the high pedestrian walkway is now closed, the bridge is used by some 40,000 people per day, and the bascules are raised around 1,000 times each year for ships passing beneath – a service that is still provided free of charge.

Above: Tower Bridge, pictured with the two bascules opening to allow ships to pass through.

Opposite, above: During a major renovation project on Tower Bridge, begun in 2008 and completed in 2012, the suspension arms — two of which are seen here — were repainted using a state-of-the-art coating system.

Opposite, below: Tower Bridge lit up at night. The bridge was fitted with a new lighting system to mark the 2012 Olympic and Paralympic Games.

Instructions

⌃ This symbol means that you should fold the pieces indicated along the indented fold lines before connecting the tabs and slots.

The two towers are constructed in the same way. In steps 1–9 the first press-out piece numbers are for the first tower and those in brackets are for the second tower.

Step 1

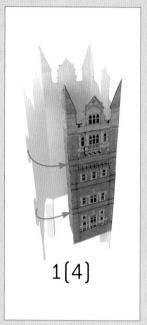

1(4)

⌃ 1, 4
Push the A (B) tabs in piece 1 (4) into the A (B) slots on piece 1 (4).

Step 2

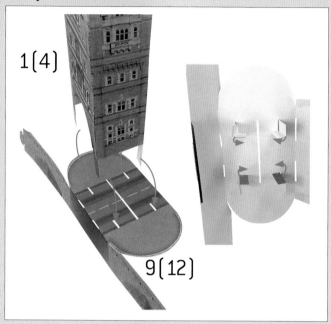

1(4)

9(12)

⌃ 9, 12
Fold the C (E) and D (F) tabs on piece 1 (4) flat and push them into the corresponding slots on piece 9 (12).
Once they are the entire way through, fold them back out to secure them in place.

Step 3

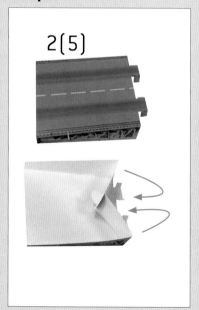

2(5)

⌃ 2, 5
Push tab K (L) on piece 2 (5) into slot K (L).

Step 4

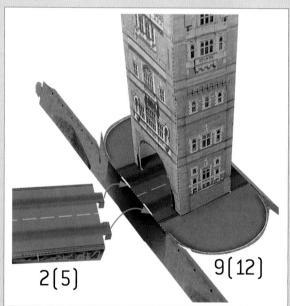

2(5)

9(12)

Fold the Q (R) tabs on piece 2 (5) back on themselves and push them into the Q (R) slots on piece 9 (12).

Step 5

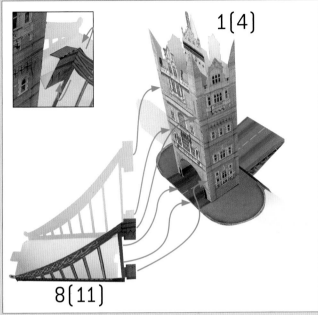

1(4)

8(11)

⚙ 8, 11
Push tabs AA (W) and AA1 (W1) on piece 8 (11) into the
corresponding slots on piece 9 (12).
Fold tabs BB, BB1, CC and CC1 on piece 8 (tabs X, X1, Y and Y1 on
piece 11) back on themselves and push them into the corresponding
slots on piece 1 (4).

Step 6

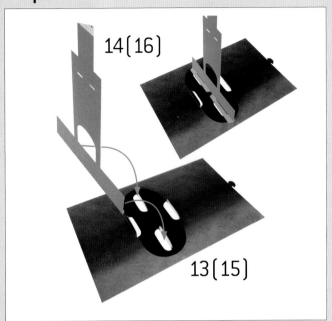

14(16)

13(15)

Fold tabs G (H) and G1 (H1) on piece 13 (15).
Fold tabs G (H) and G1 (H1) on piece 14 (16).
Push tabs G (H) and G1 (H1) on piece 13 (15) into slots G (H) and
G1 (H1) on piece 14 (16).

Step 7

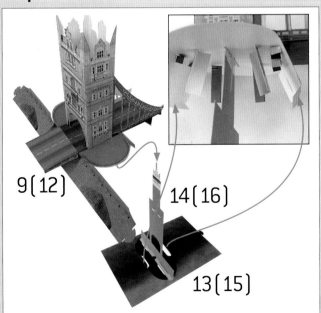

9(12)

14(16)

13(15)

Fold tabs P (O) and M (N) on piece 13 (15).
Push piece 14 (16) up into slot J (I) on piece 9 (12).
Fold tabs P (O) and M (N) on piece 9 (12).
Push tabs P (O) and M (N) on piece 13 (15) up into the
corresponding slots on piece 9 (12).

Step 8

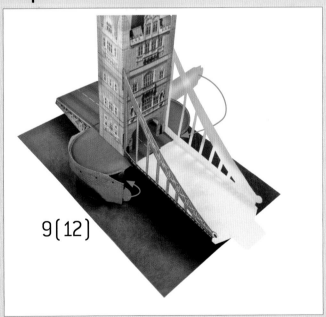

9(12)

Push tabs LL (NN) and KK (MM) on piece 9 (12) into the
corresponding slots on piece 9 (12).

Step 9

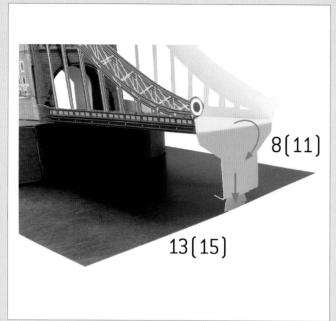

8 (11)

13 (15)

Fold the support section of piece 8 (11) down to a 90-degree angle. Fold tab DD (Z) on piece 13 (15) and push it into slot DD (Z) on piece 8 (11).

Step 10

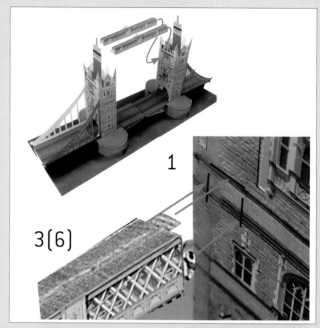

1

3 (6)

⏿ 3, 6

Push the S tabs on piece 3 into the S slots on piece 1.
Push the U tabs on piece 6 into the U slots on piece 1.

Step 11

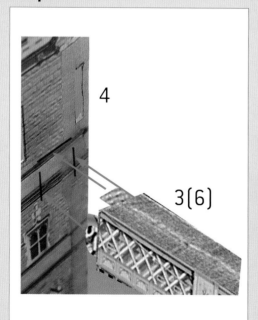

4

3 (6)

Push the T tabs on piece 3 into the T slots on piece 4.
Push the V tabs on piece 6 into the V slots on piece 4.

Step 12

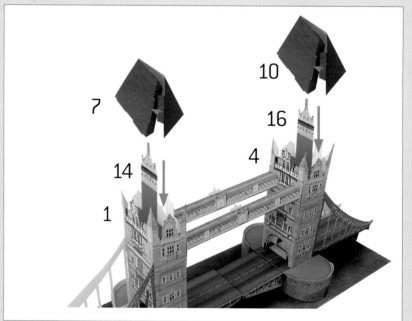

10

7

16

4

14

1

⏿ 7, 10

Push tab HH on piece 7 into slot HH on piece 7. Fold tabs II and JJ on piece 7 flat.
Push tab EE on piece 10 into slot EE on piece 10. Fold tabs FF and GG on piece 10 flat.
Push piece 7 onto piece 14 and push the II and JJ tabs on the top of piece 1 into the corresponding slots on piece 7.
Push piece 10 onto piece 16 and push the FF and GG tabs on the top of piece 4 into the corresponding slots on piece 10.

All of the press-out pages in this section of the book are perforated near the gutter of the book. Please DO NOT tear along the perforat[e]
line until after you have removed all of the press-out pieces from the page, otherwise you may damage the press-out pieces.

D1

7

E1

F1

G1

H1

I1

J1

K1

D

3

E

F

G

H

5

I

J

K

6

DD

2

BB   BB

FF

EE

GG

CC   CC

BB   BB

R   Q

1

Q

Q

R   Q

R   Q

R   Q

R   Q

R   Q

R   Q

R   Q

R   Q

8

CC   CC

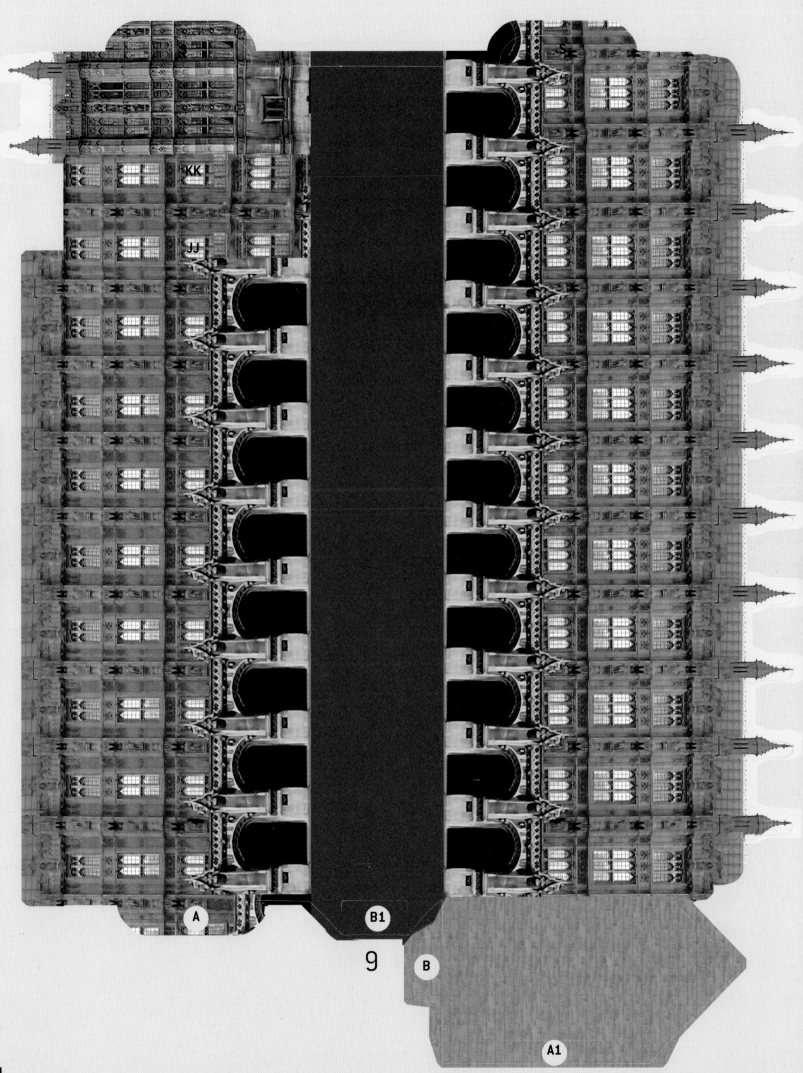

KK

JJ

S

A

B1

9

B

A1

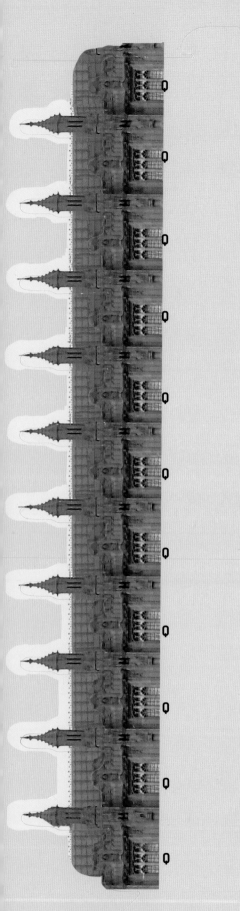

S

Q

Q

R

Q

Q

KK

Q

JJ

Q

R

Q

R

9

Q

R

Q

R

Q

R

Q

R

Q

R

Q

R

Q

R

B1

A

B

A1

PP   PP   PP   PP

10

QQ   QQ   QQ   QQ   QQ   QQ

MM   LL

II 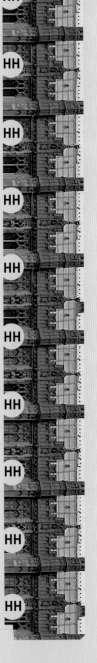 HH

II   HH

II   HH

II   HH

II   HH

11

II   HH

II   HH

II   HH

II   HH

II   HH

KK   JJ

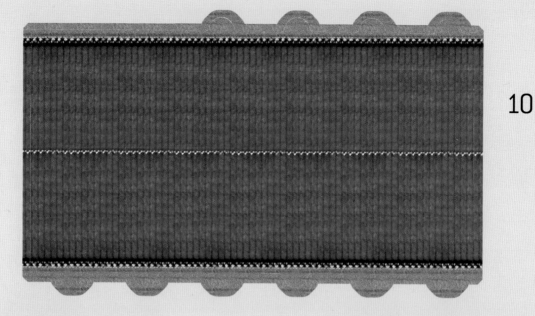

10

11

LL

MM

JJ

KK

BIG BEN AND THE HOUSES OF PARLIAMENT

L1

O1

N1

O1

N1

M1

L1

M1

L2

N2

N2

M2

O2

N2

M2

O2

D2

E2

C

F2

G2

H2

I2

J2

K2

C1

12

C1

C

C

C1

S

S

C1

P1

P1

P1

P

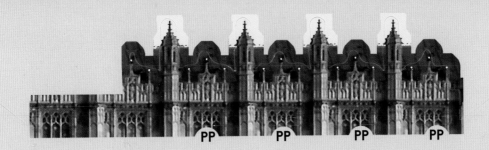

PP　　PP　　PP　　PP

NN

SS　　RR

TT

13

NN

TT

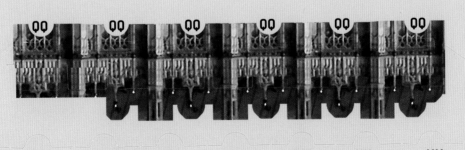

QQ　　QQ　　QQ　　QQ　　QQ　　QQ

HH　　HH　　HH　　HH　　HH　　HH　　HH　　HH　　HH　　HH

14

II　　II　　II　　II　　II　　II　　II　　II　　II　　II

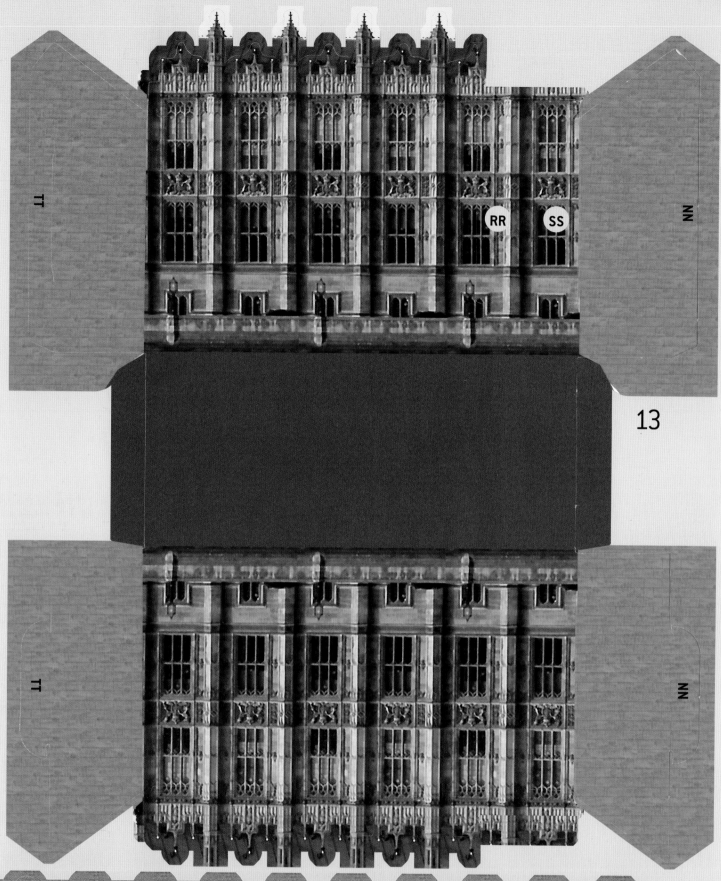

RR SS

TT

NN

13

TT

NN

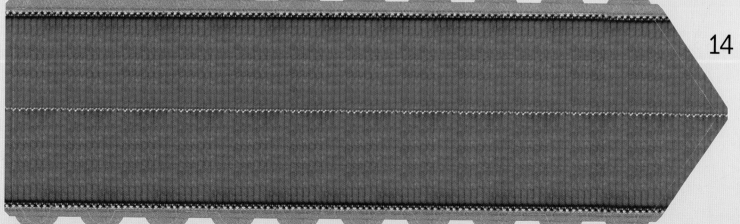

14

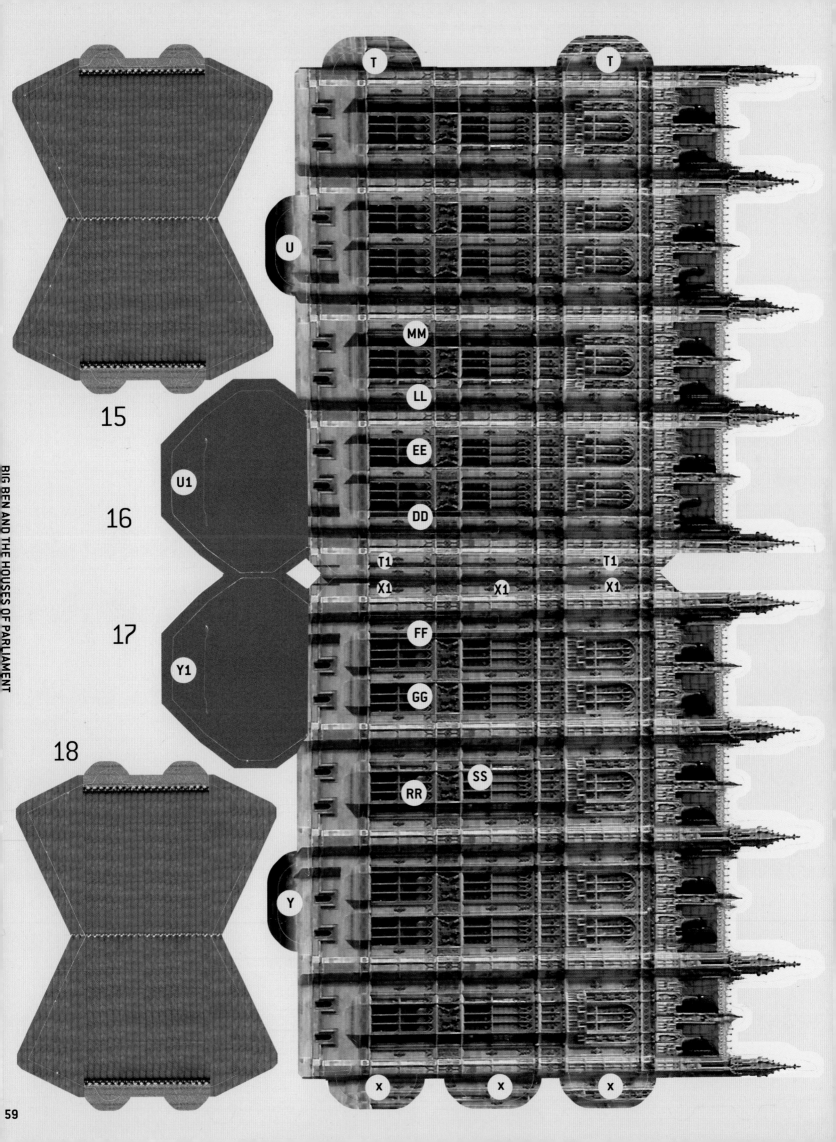

15

16

17

18

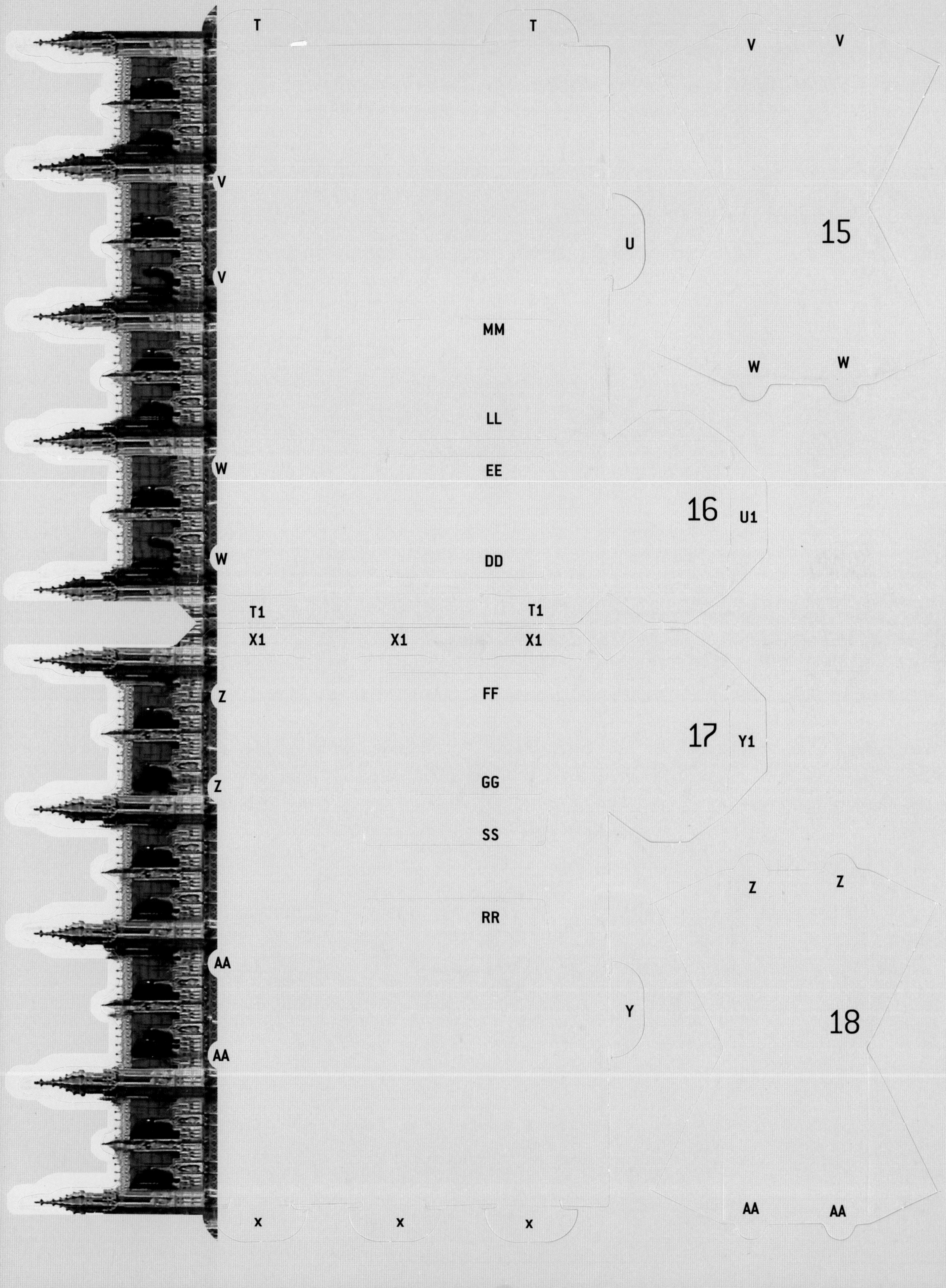

T T V V

15

X X X U

V

V MM

LL

W EE

W 16 U1

W DD

T1 T1

X1 X1 X1

Z FF

Z 17 Y1

GG

SS

Z Z

RR

AA

Y

AA 18

X X X AA AA

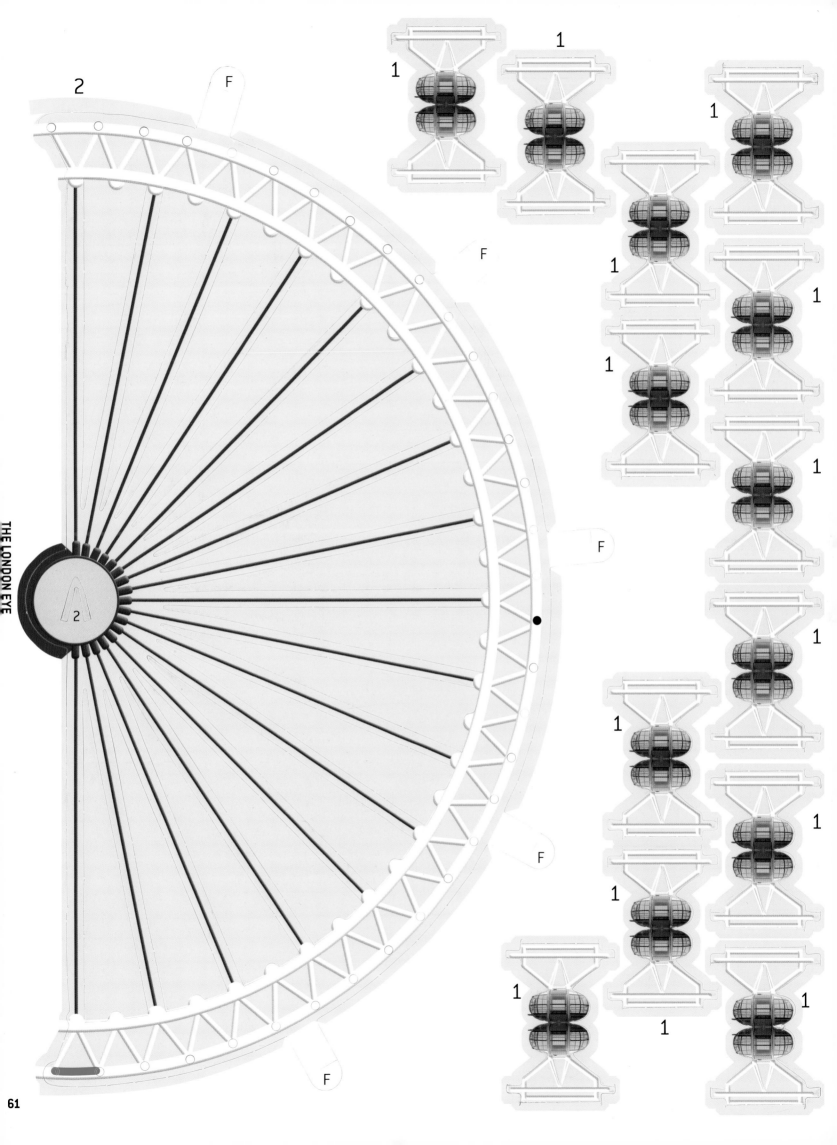

2

F

F

F

F

F

1

1

1

1

1

1

1

1

1

1

1

1

1

1

1

1

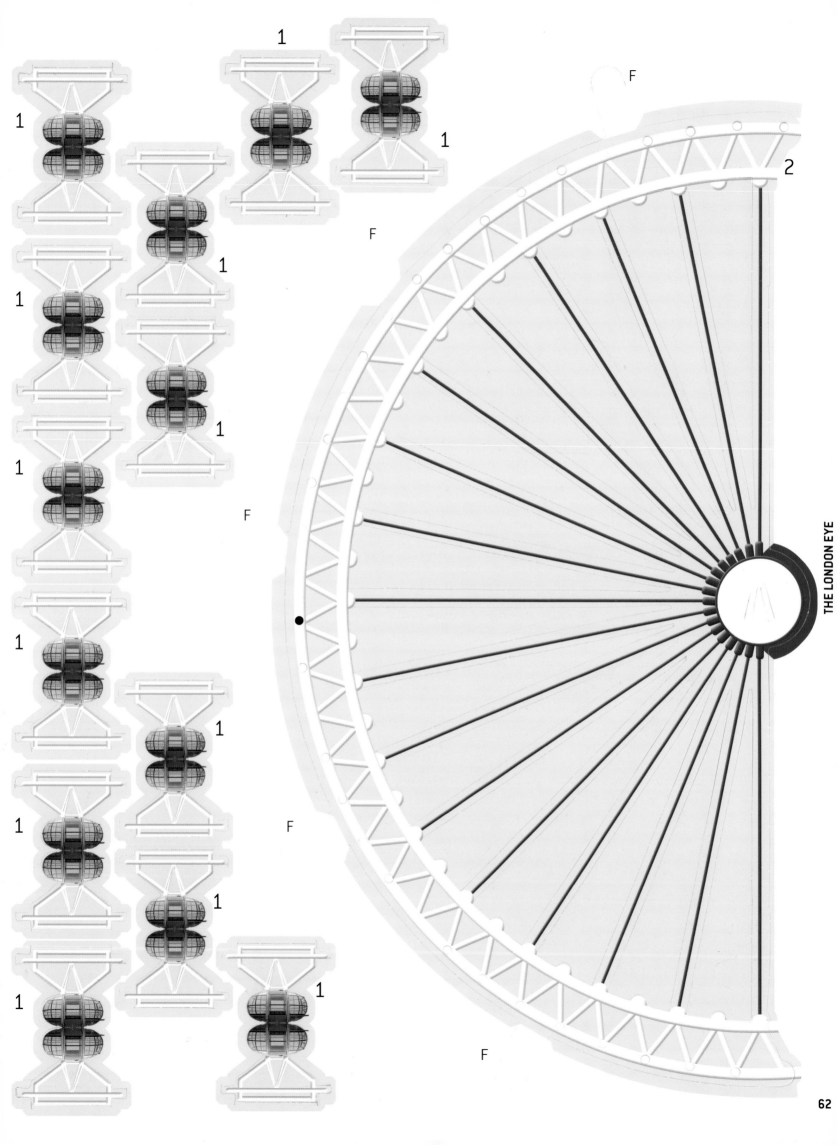

1

1

1

1

1

1

1

1

1

1

1

1

1

1

F

F

F

F

F

2

THE LONDON EYE

62

F

3

F

1

F

1

1

1

1

F

1

1

F

1

1

F

1

1

F

1

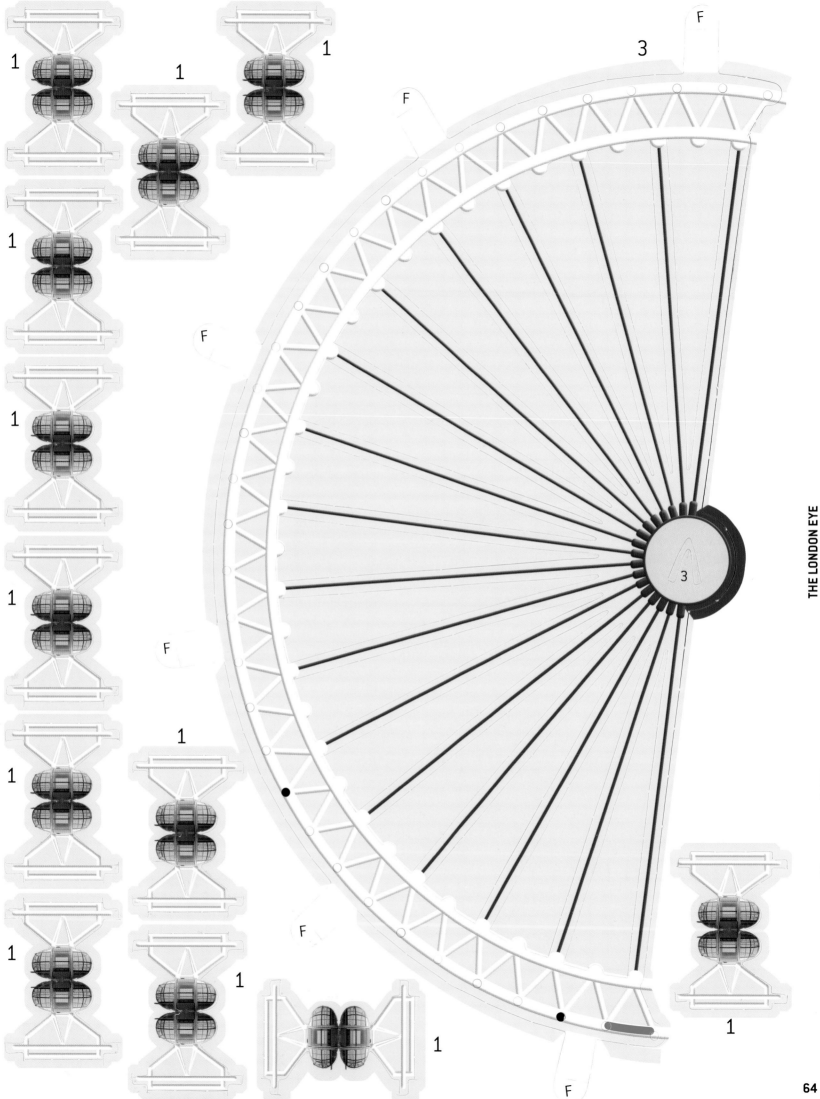

1
1
1
1
1
1
1
1
1
1
1
1
1
1

3
F
F
F
F
F

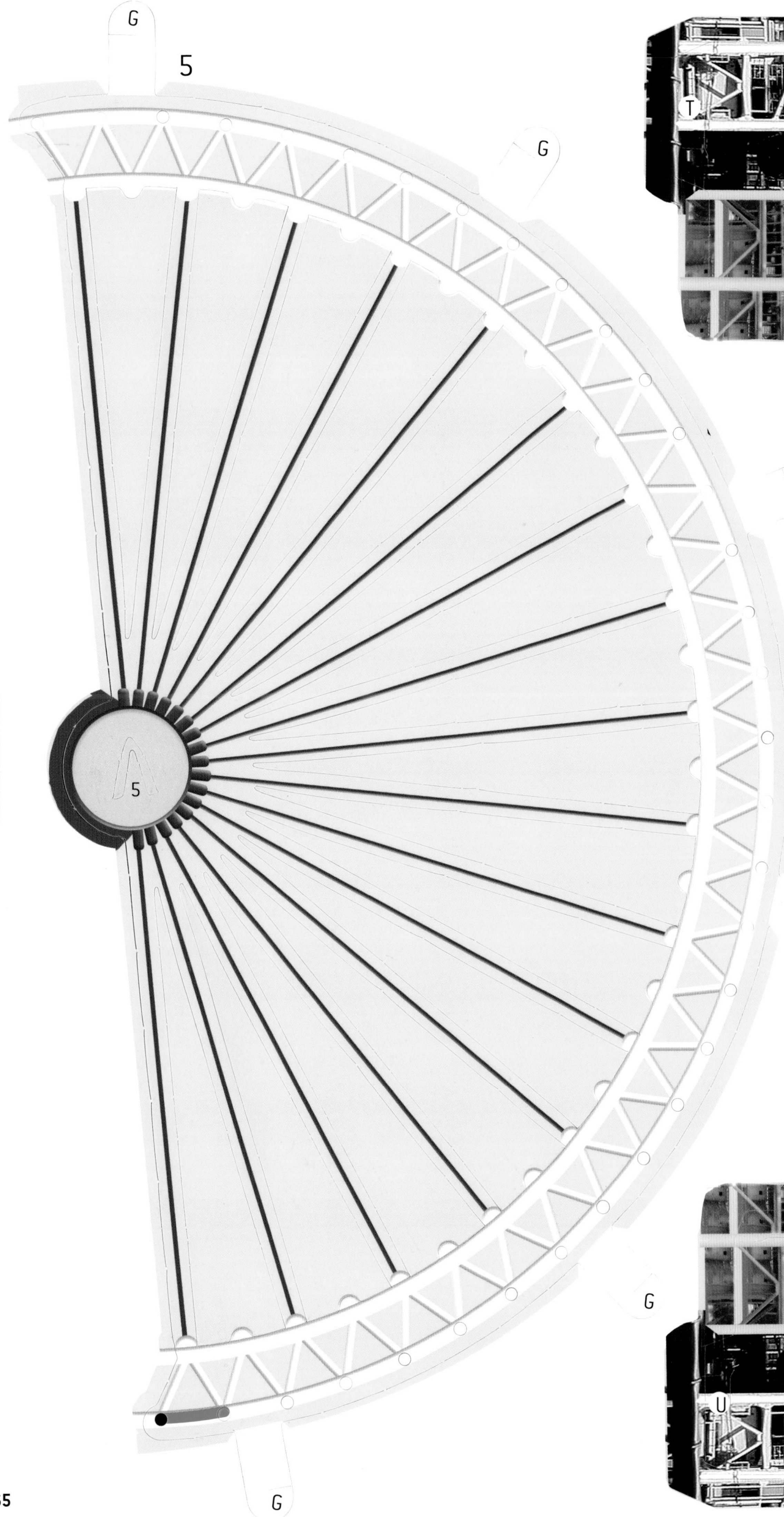

G

5

G

G

G

5

G

G

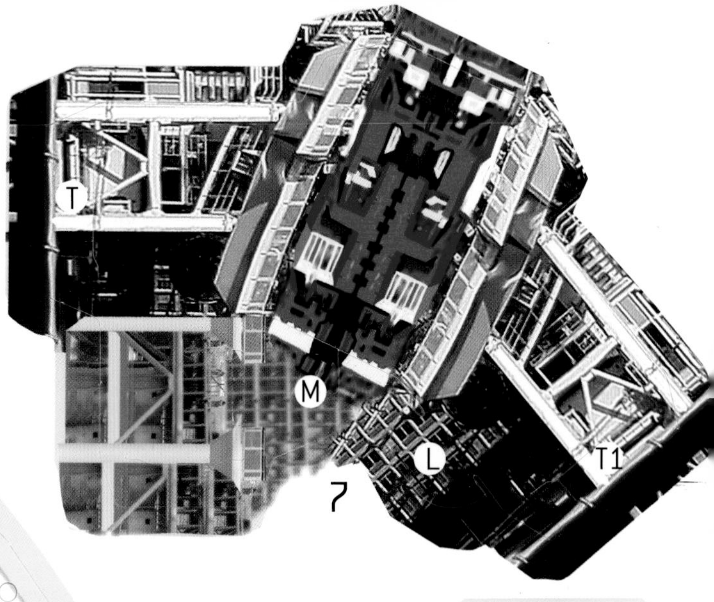

G

7

T

M

L

T1

1

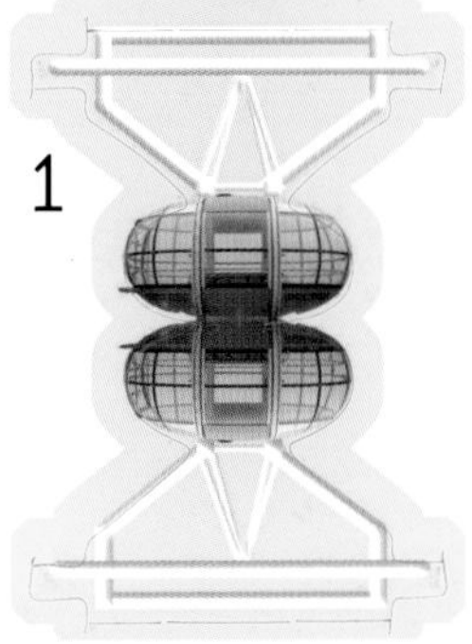

1

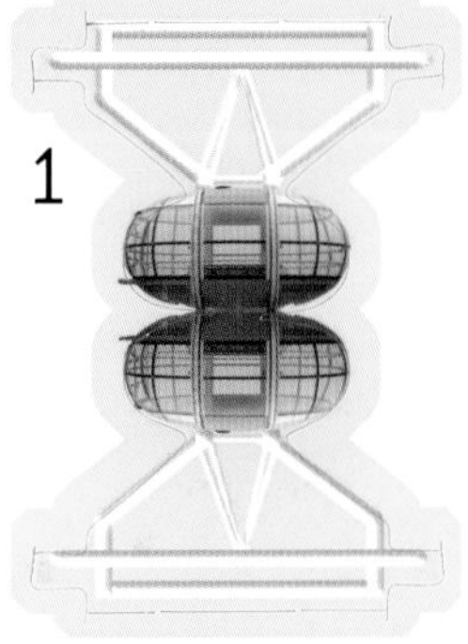

1

8

N

U1

O

G

U

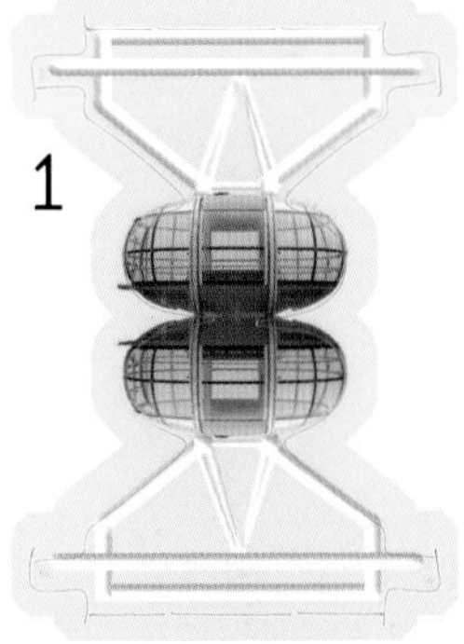

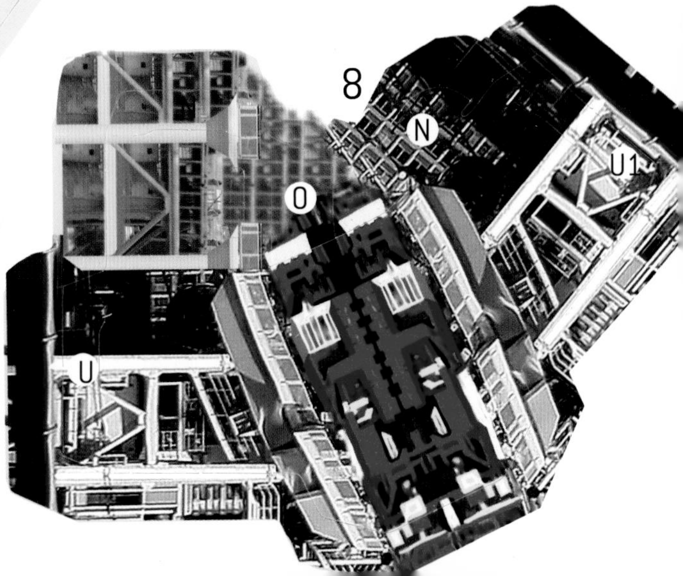

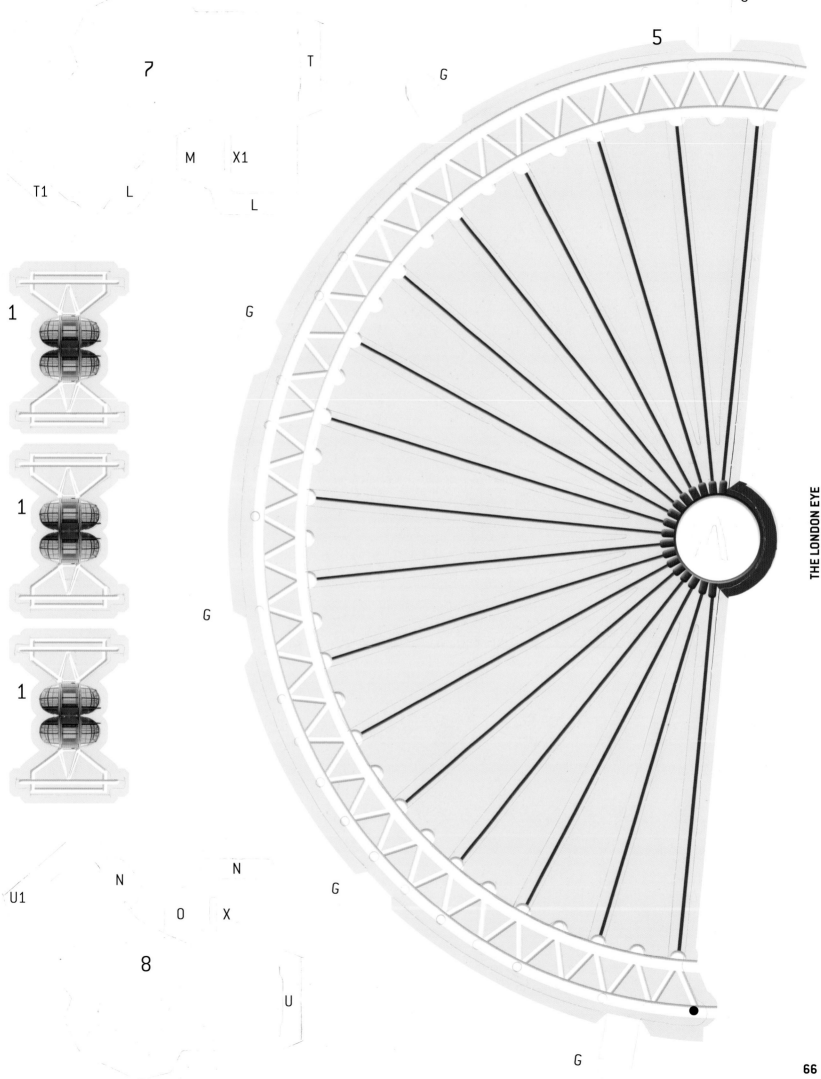

7

T

G

G

5

G

M X1

T1 L L

G

1

1

G

1

N N

U1 O X

8

U

G

G

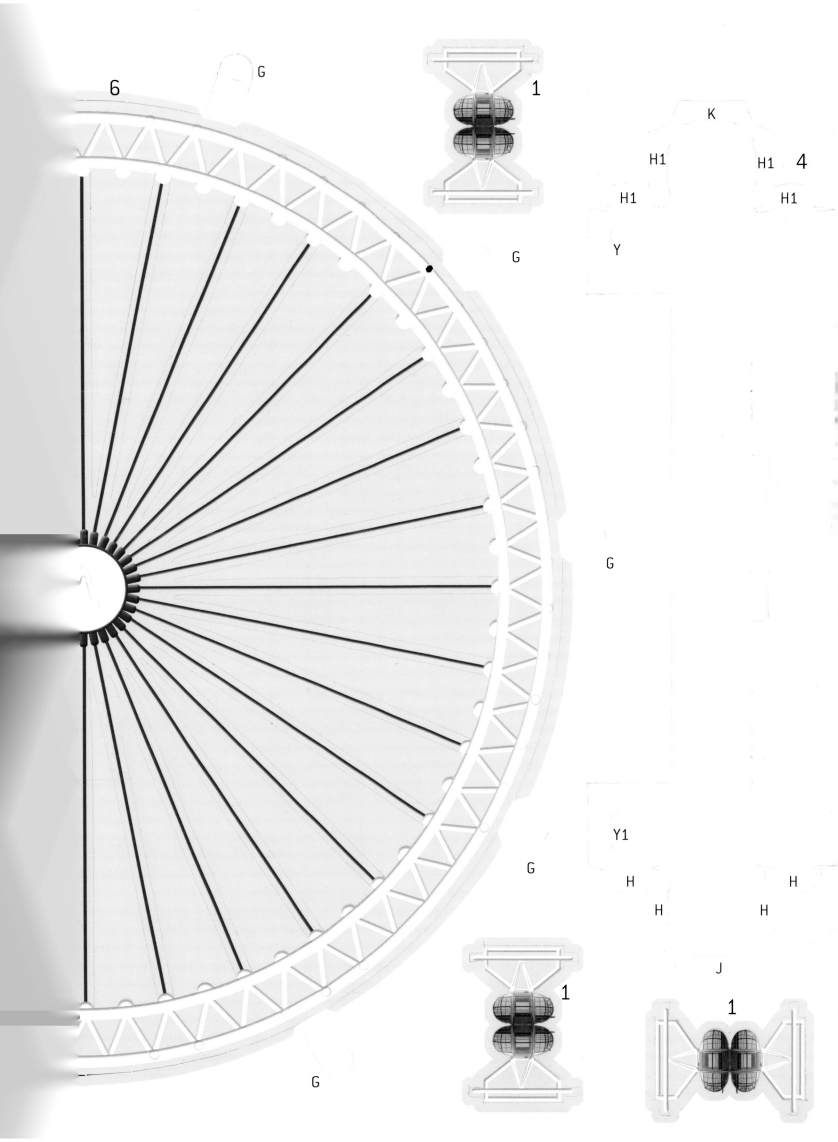

6

G

1

K

H1 H1 4

H1   H1

G

Y

G

G

Y1

G

H   H

H   H

J

1

1

G

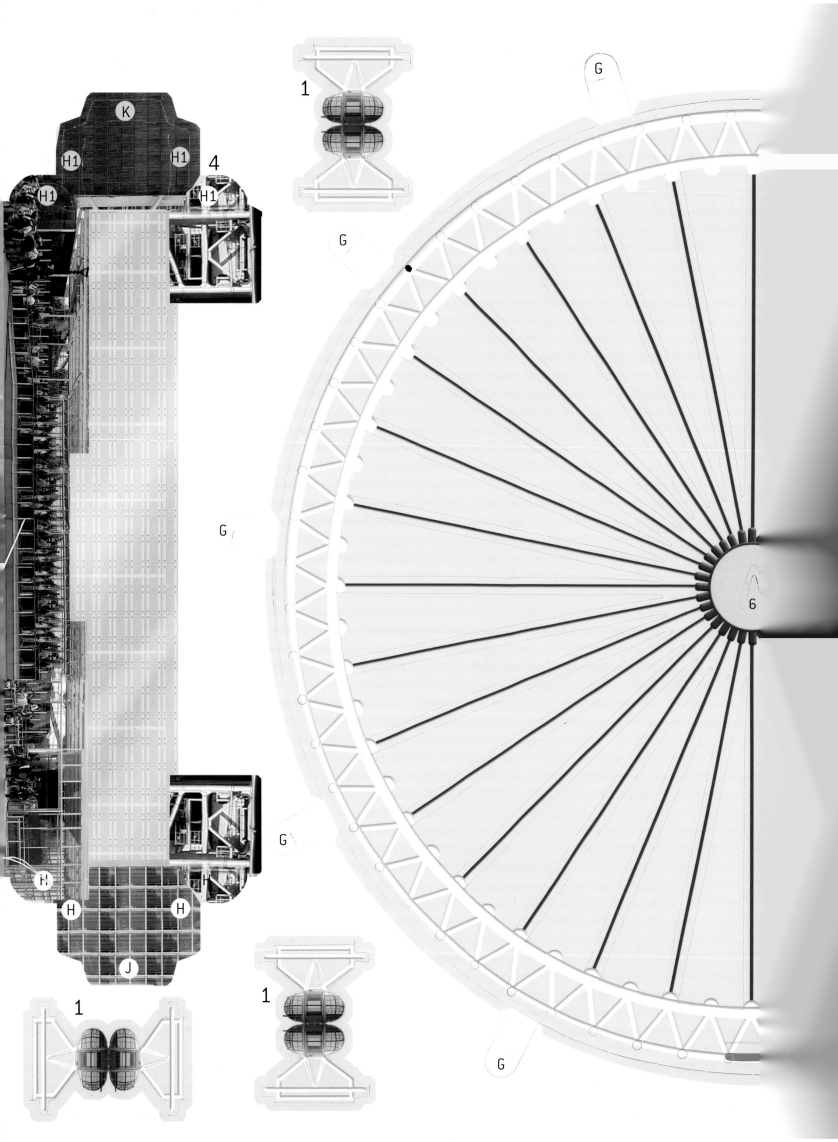

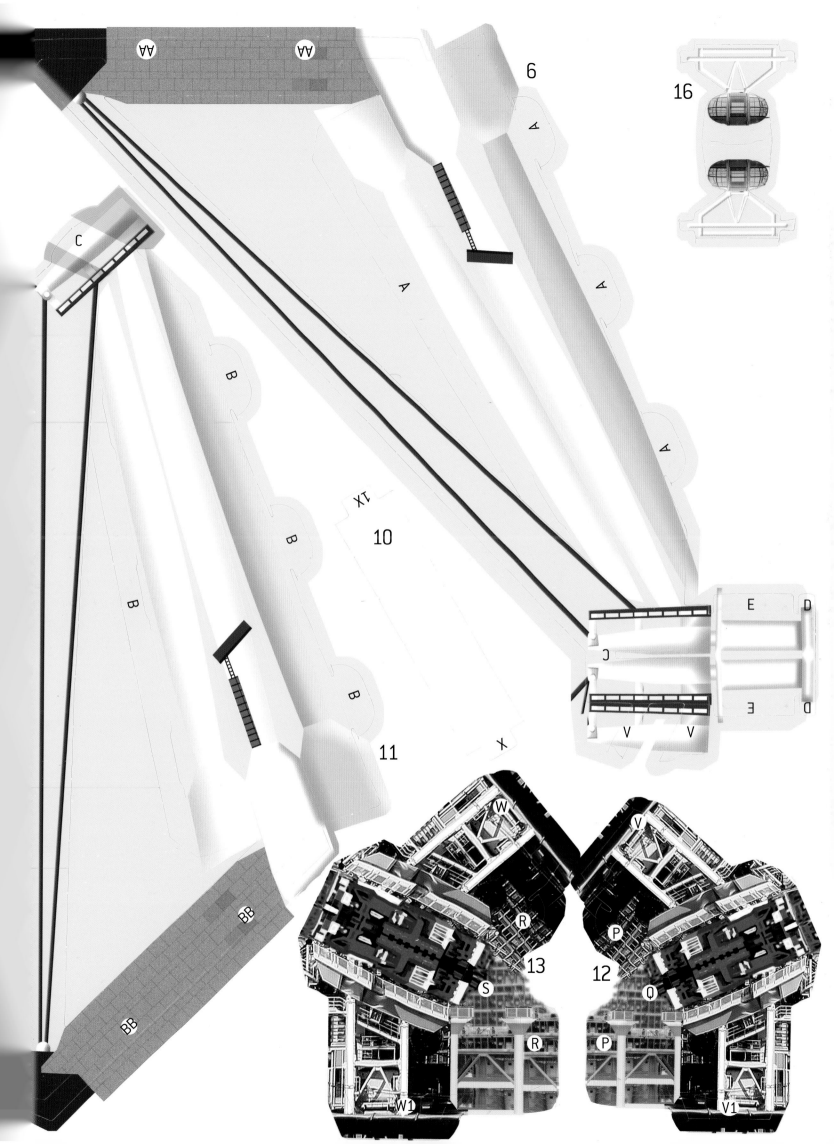

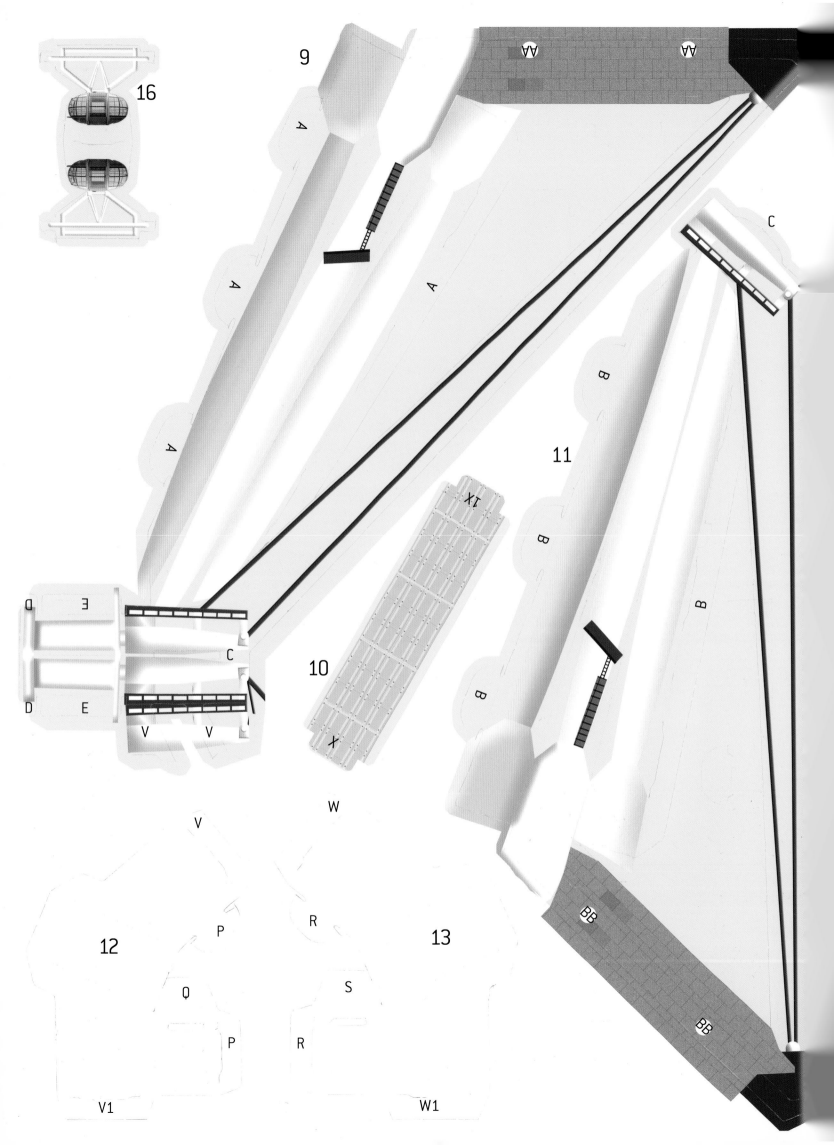

Z   Z   Z

14

Z   Z   Z

BB   15   AA

BB   AA

THE LONDON EYE

Y   Y1

BB   AA

K   J

U   T

U1   T1

W   V

W1   V1

BB

UU

TT

UU

VV

3

XX

VV

YY

WW

VV

YY

WW

TT

1

VV

2

YY

WW

TT

VV

YY

WW

TT

VV

W

YY

WW

TT

Z

VV

W

YY

WW

TT

VV

Y

X

YY

WW

TT

X

VV

YY

WW

TT

VV

YY

WW

TT

VV

XX

TT

AA

UU

VV

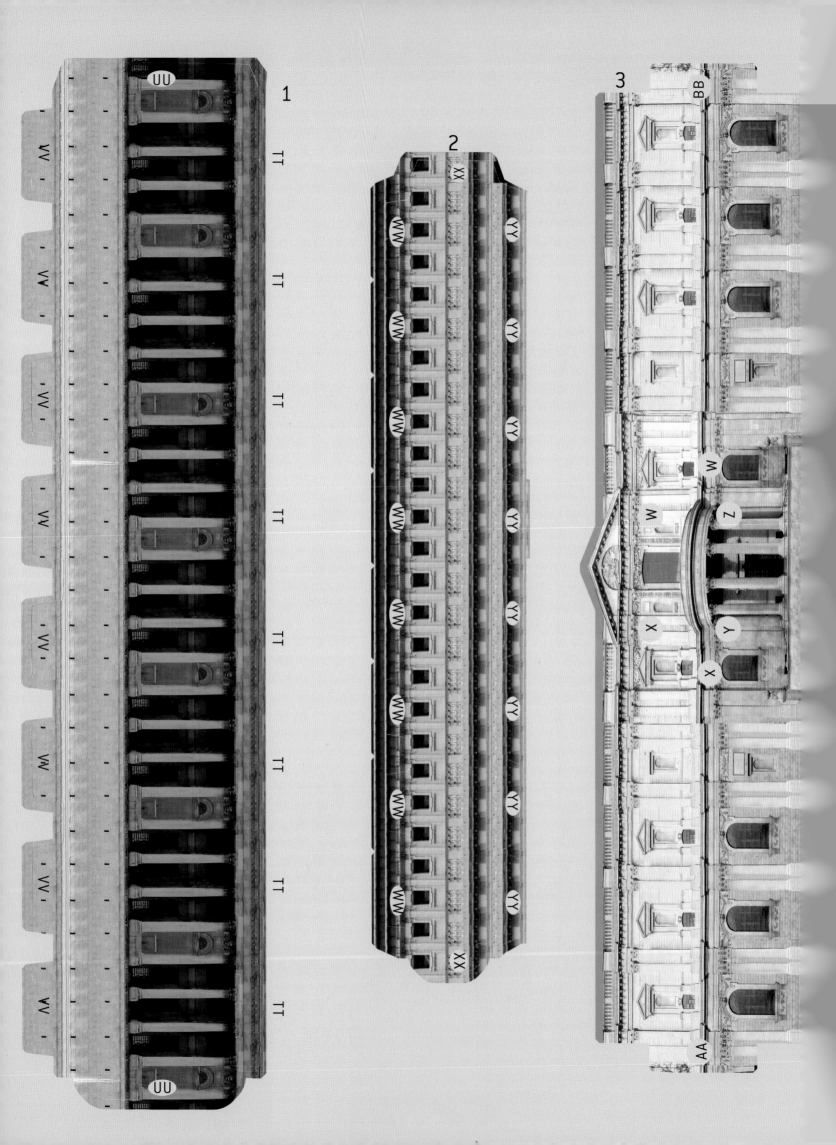

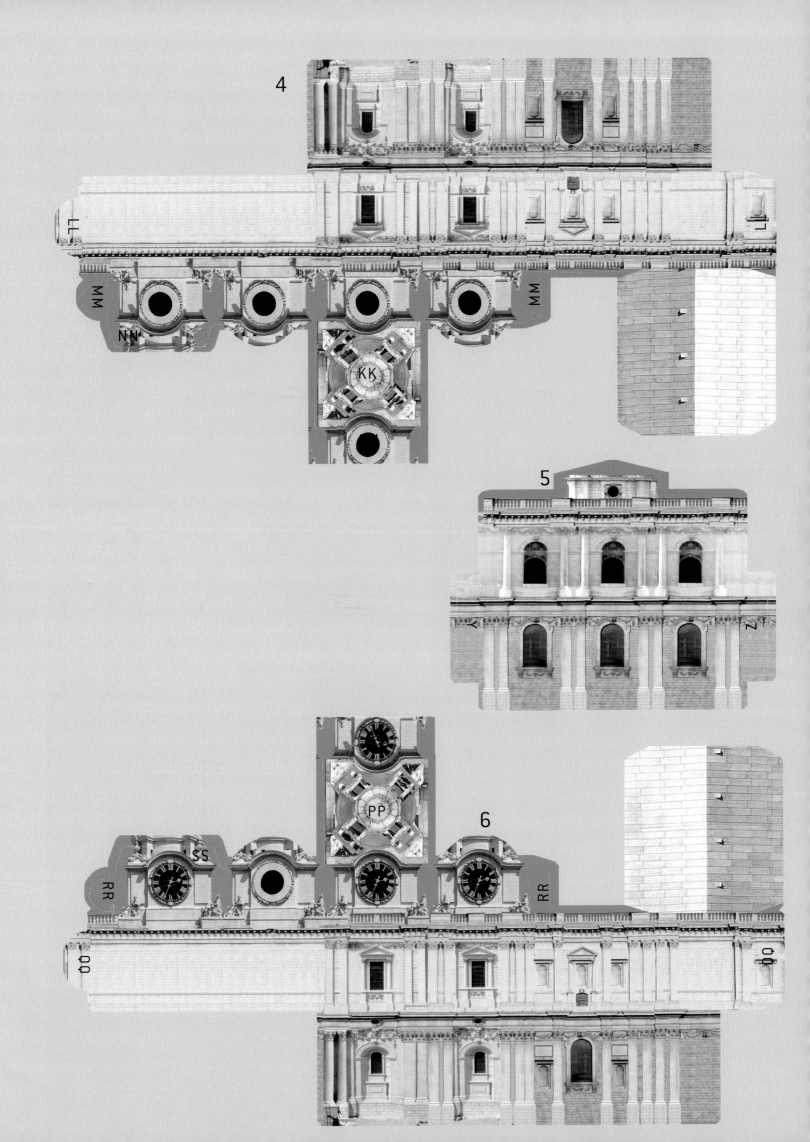

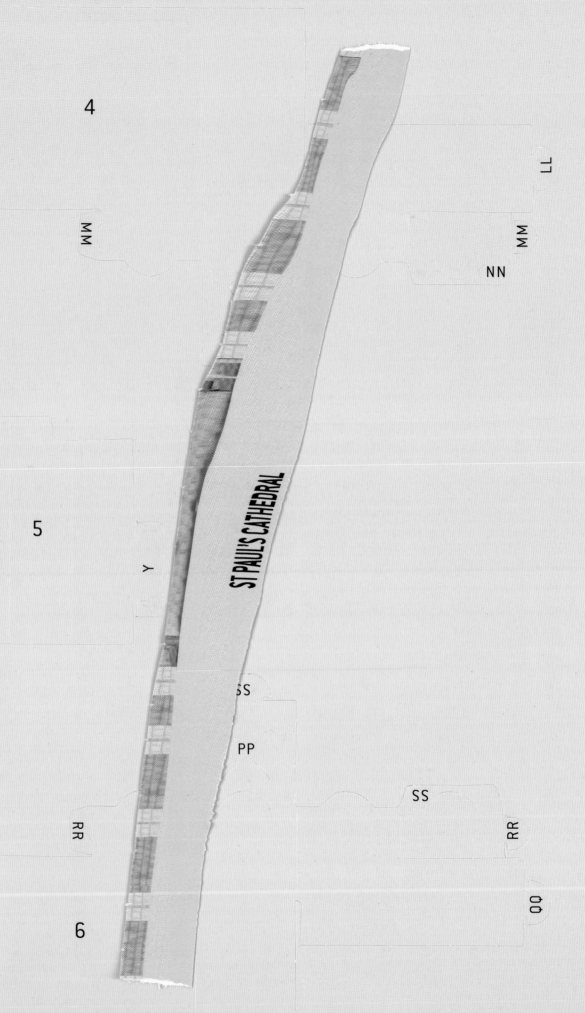

ST PAUL'S CATHEDRAL

4

LL

MM

NN

LL

MM

5

Z

Y

SS

PP

SS

RR

RR

OO

6

OO

P P O O T

8

R R Q Q

R

X X W W M R

N1 M1 N 7

Q

9

Q

S

V V U U

G G H H

10

J J I I

J I

K J I 11

E1

F1 F

E

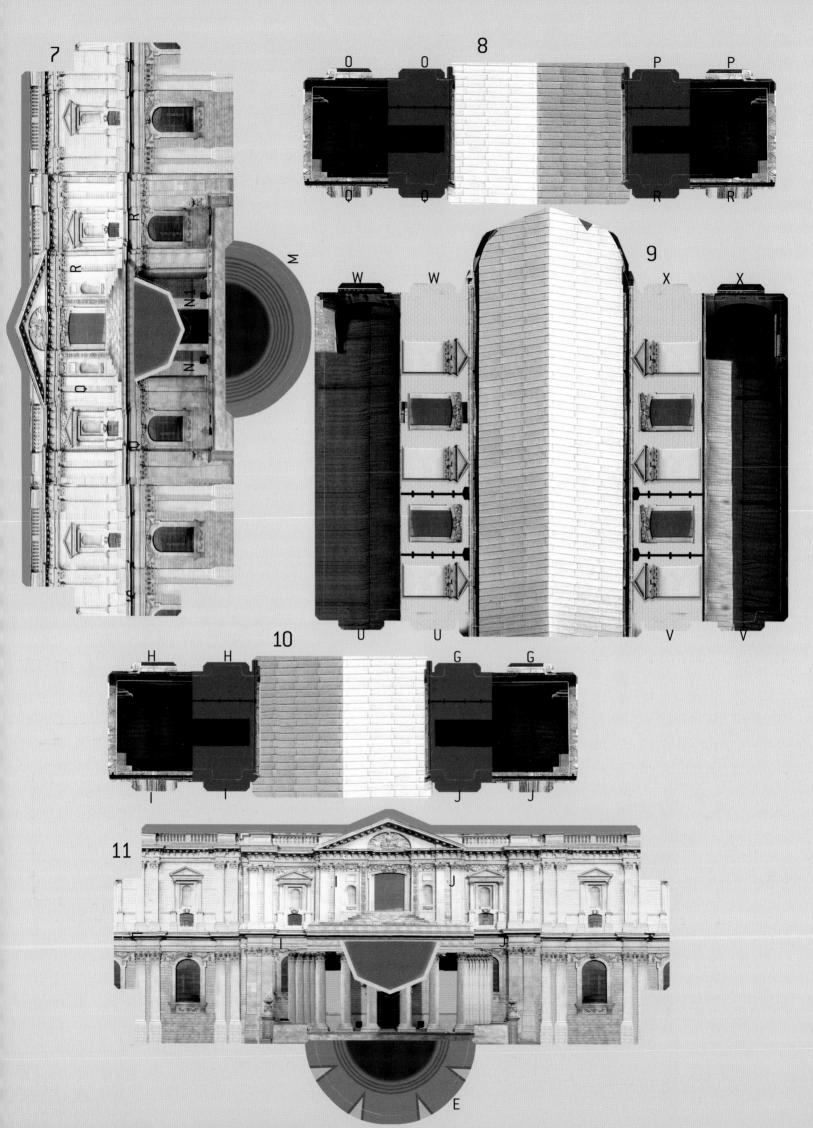

7

8

O O P P

Q Q R R

M

N N

R

R

R

W W X X

9

U U V V

10

H H G G

I I J J

11

I J

I J

M

E

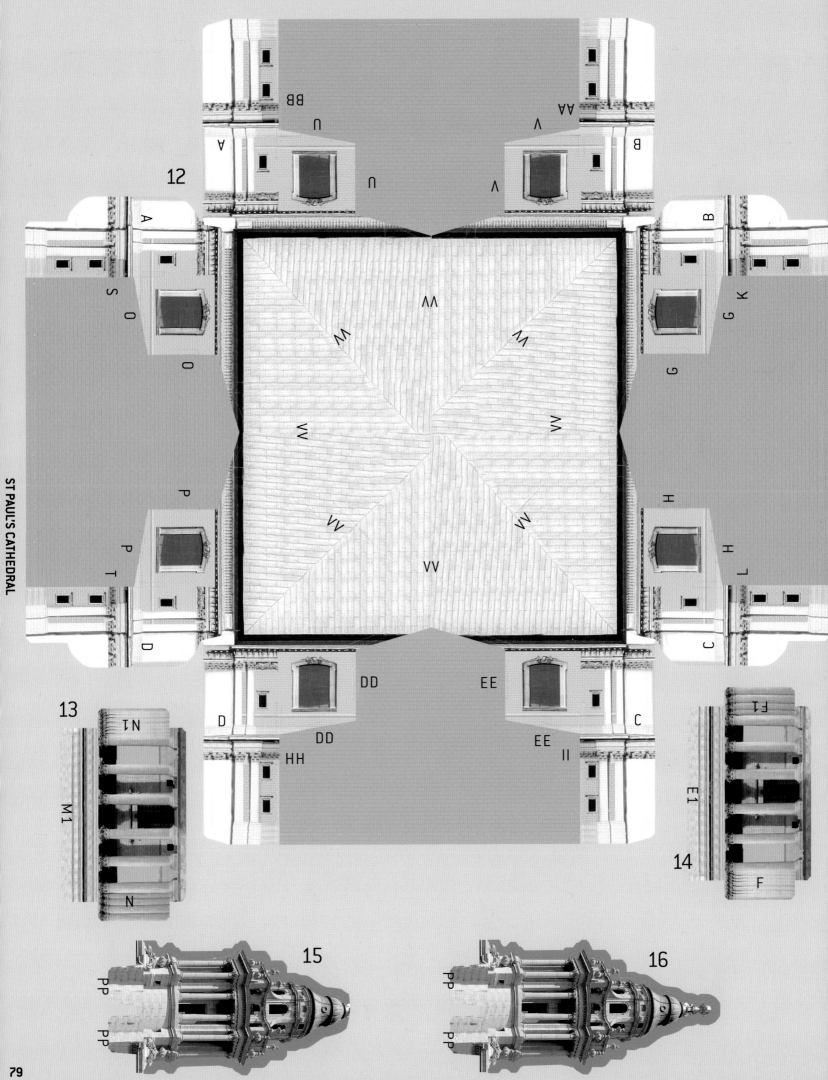

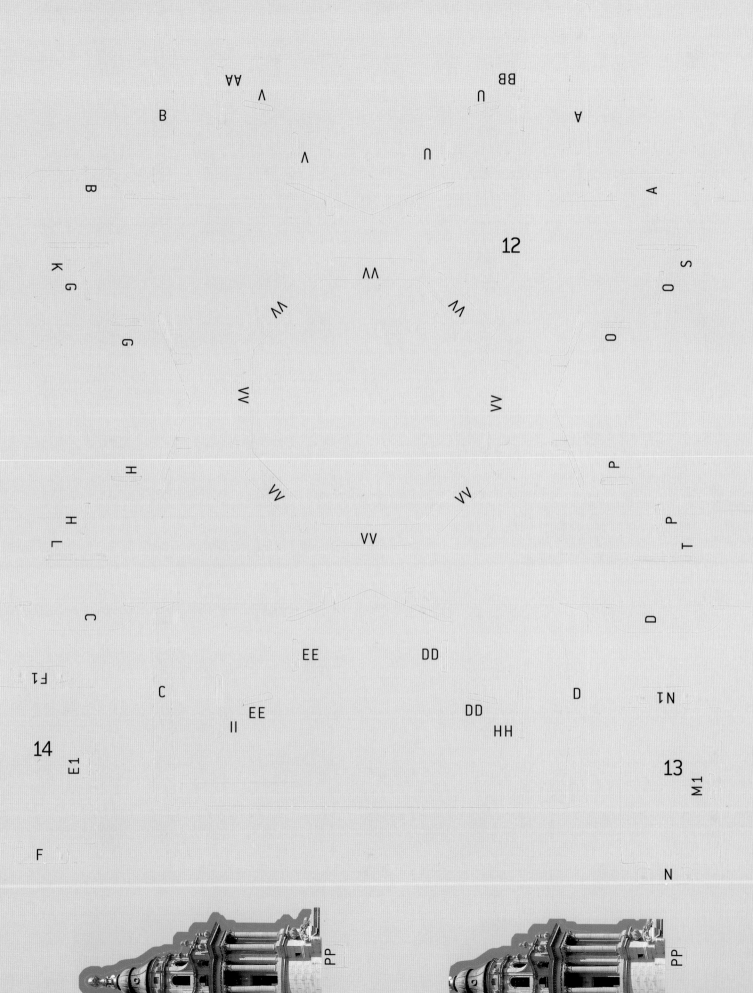

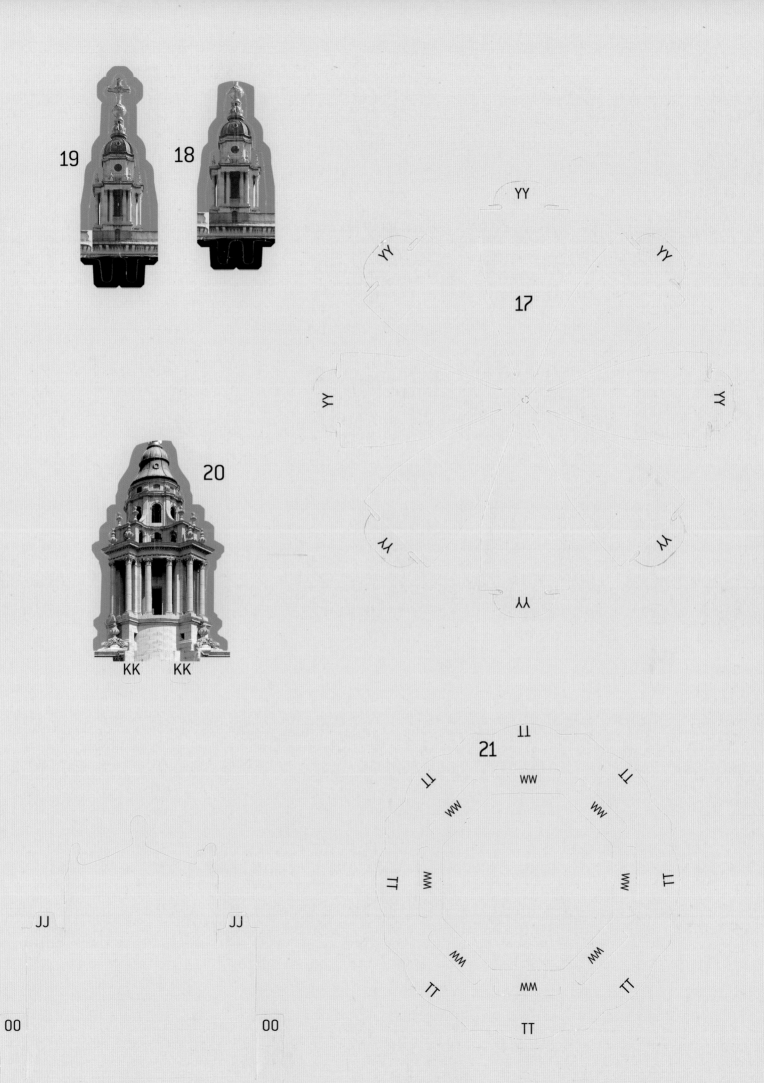

19 18

17

YY
YY
YY
YY
YY
YY
YY
YY

20

KK KK

21

TT
TT WW TT
WW WW
WW MM MM WW
TT TT
MM MM
TT MM MM TT
MM
TT

JJ JJ

OO OO

22

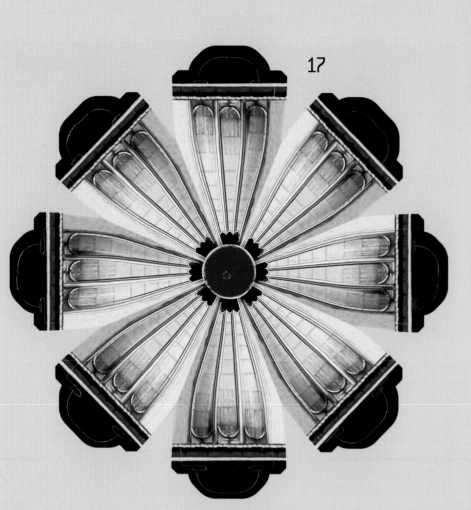

17

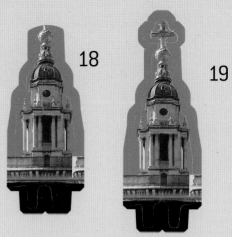

18

19

20

KK   KK

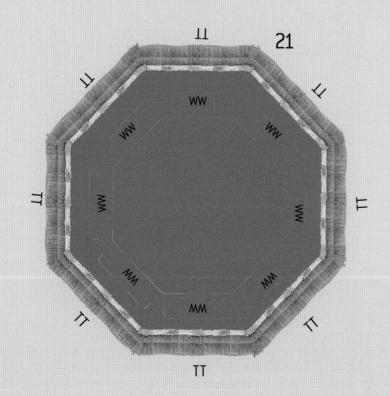

21

TT

TT

WW

WW   WW

TT   WW

MM   WW

TT   MM   MM

MM

TT   MM

TT   TT

TT

JJ   JJ

OO   OO

22

23

CC

GG

GG

CC

LOCATE PIECE 6 HERE

II

24

HH

LOCATE PIECE 4 HERE

FF

FF

26

DD

DD

EE

EE

25

KK

KK

FF

FF

GG

GG

LOCATE PIECE 6 HERE

GG

CC

II

23

JJ

GG

CC

LOCATE PIECE 4 HERE

CC

FF

JJ

FF

24

HH

CC

EE

EE

DD

DD

26

25

KK

KK

GG

GG

FF

FF

P1 P

24

SS

C1 C

A
A1
B1

1

2

D1 D

B

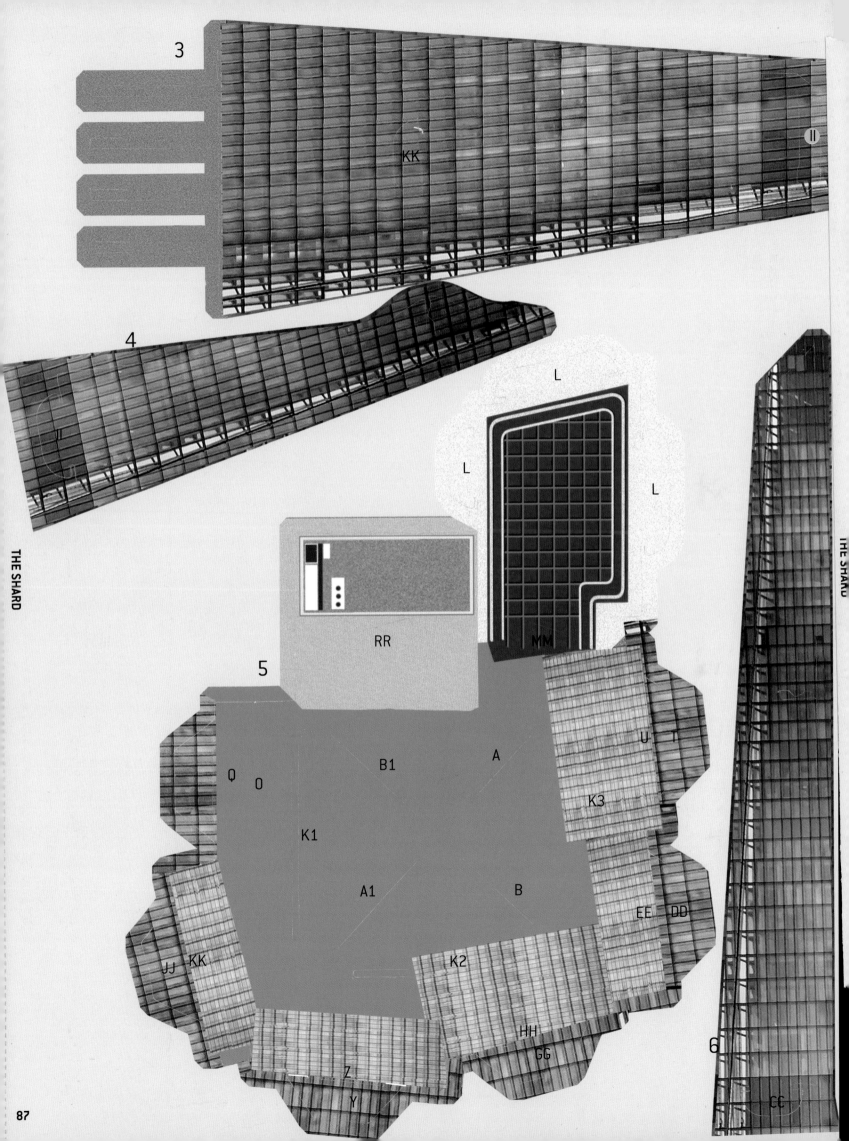

II

3

KK

4

II

L

L

L

MM

RR

T   U

A

B1

5

Q   O

K3

K1

B

A1

DD   EE

K2

KK   JJ

6

HH

GG

Z

CC

Y

P

8

O

HH

M1

W

S

BB

11

10

FF

9

FF

M

M1

X1

X

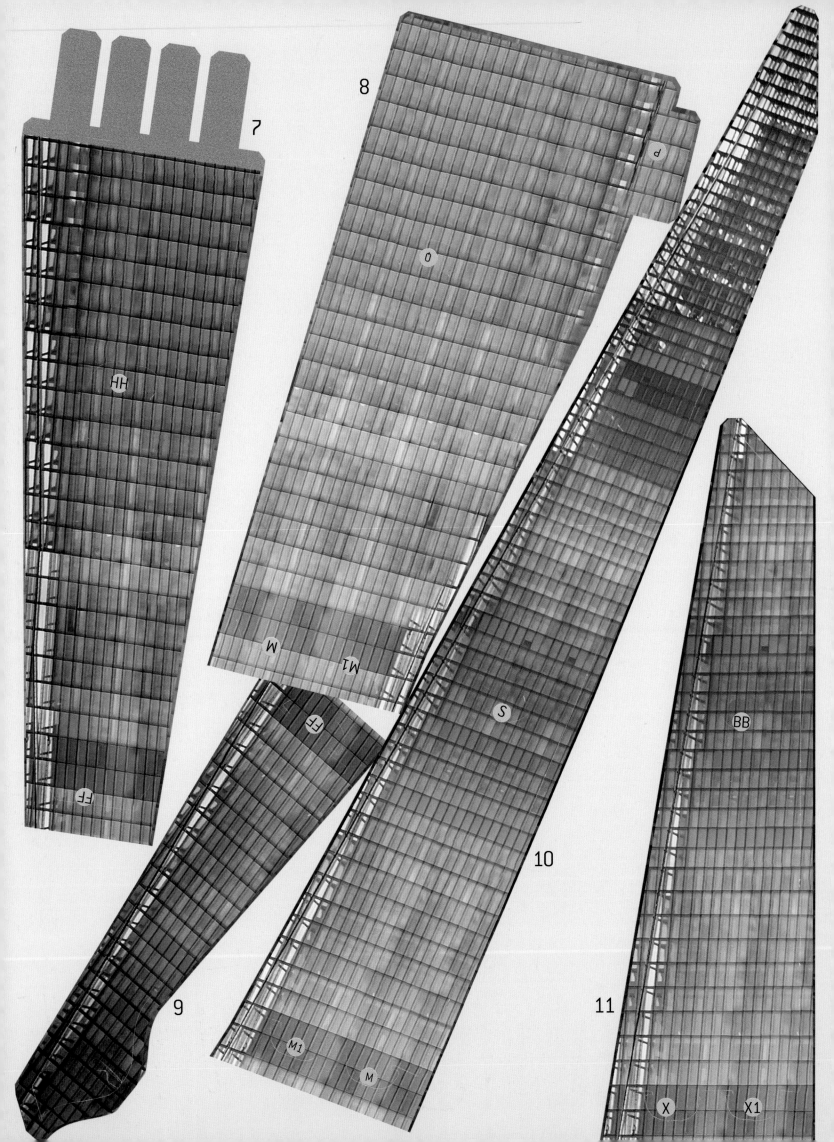

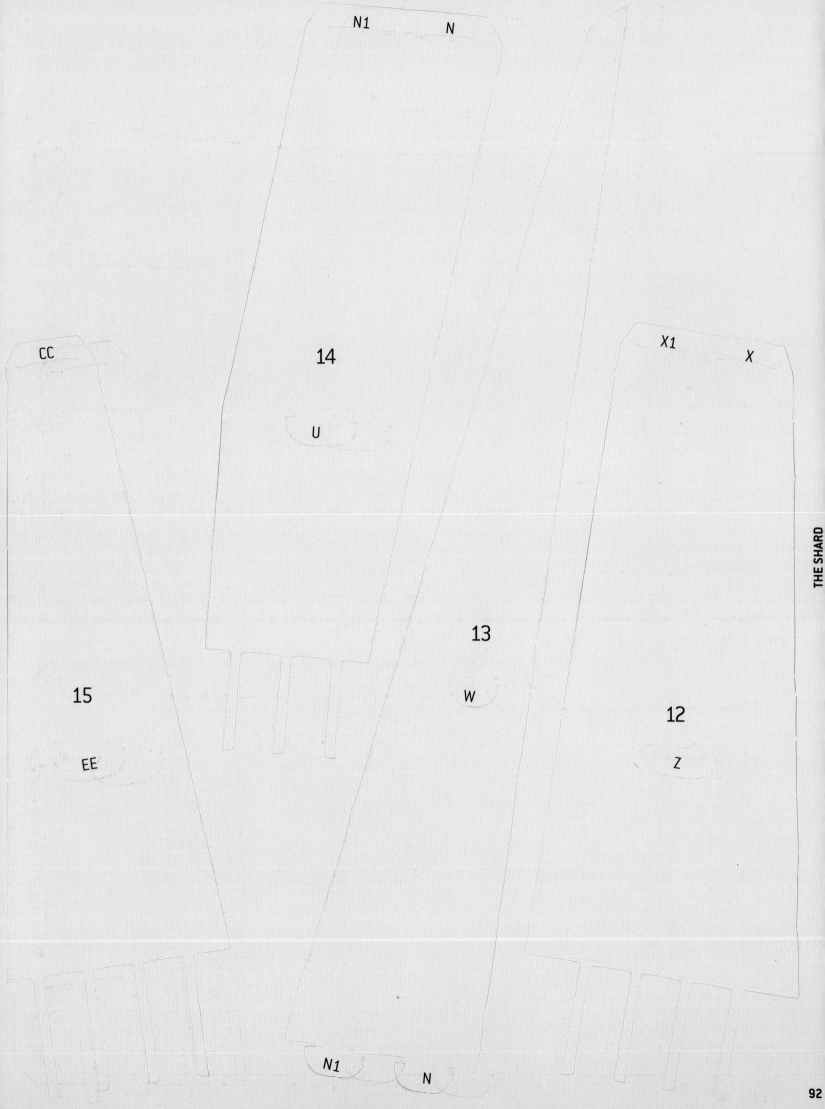

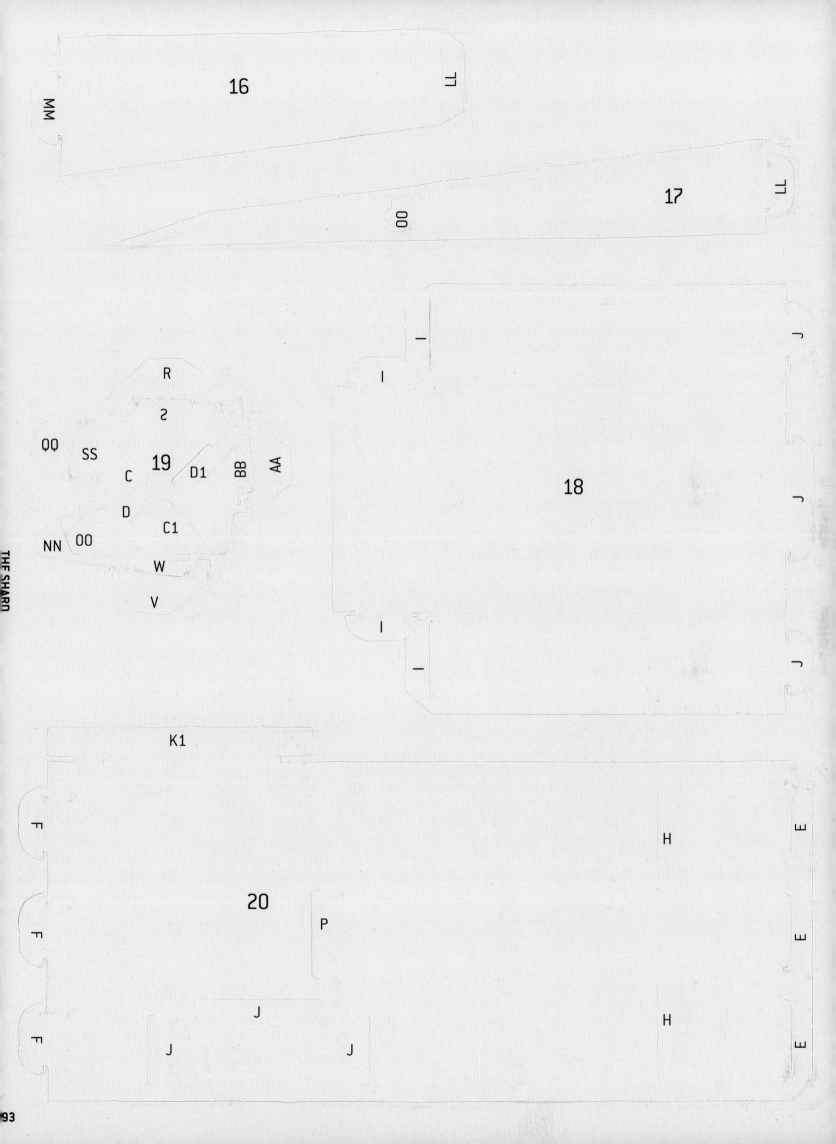

16

MM

LL

17

LL

OO

I

I

R

2

QQ

SS

19

C

D1

BB

AA

18

J

J

J

I

I

D

OO

C1

NN

W

V

K1

F

E

H

F

20

P

E

J

F

J

J

H

E

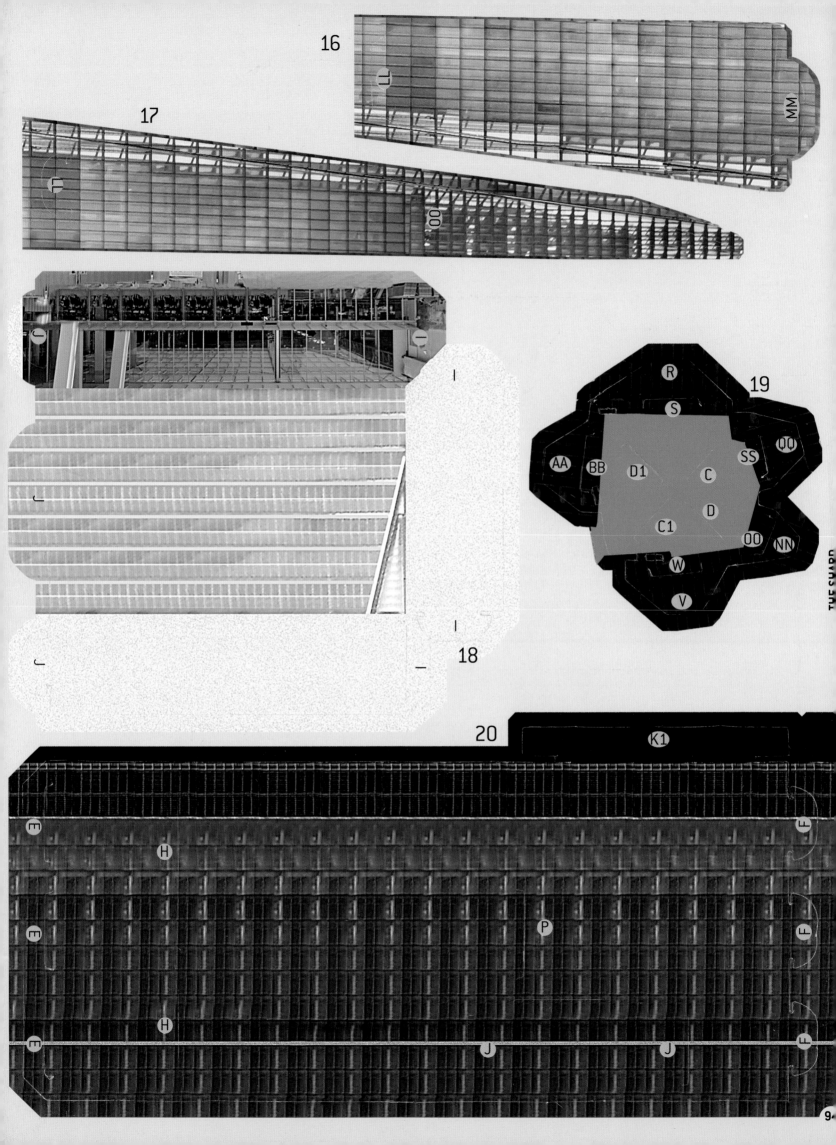

16

17

LL

MM

OO

J

I

I

J

18

J

I

19

R

S

AA BB D1 C

C1 D

W OO NN

V

SS QQ

THE SHARD

20

K1

E F

H

E P F

H

E J J F

9.

23

21

22

RR

P

P1

L L L

G H

G H

K2 K3

F E

G

F E

F

G E

23

P
P1

RR

21

L   L   L

H   G

H   G

22

K3   K2

E
G
E
E
G
E

F
F
F

U
U U
S
S S

A   A

                                        BB   CC

                          1

A   A

                                        BB1   CC1

D   D   C   K   C   K

                                                            Q   Q

                                                                            2

T   S

T   3   S

T   S

II II JJ JJ

S S U U

A

A

A

A

1

K K

C C D D

Q Q

2

S T

S T 3

S T

FF FF GG GG

V V V T T

B B

B B

4

F F E E L

L

R R

5

6 U U V

U V

GG   GG   FF   FF

T   V
T   T   V   V

B   B

X   Y

4

B   B

X1   Y1

L   E   L   E   F   F

R   R

5

V   U

V   6   U

V   U

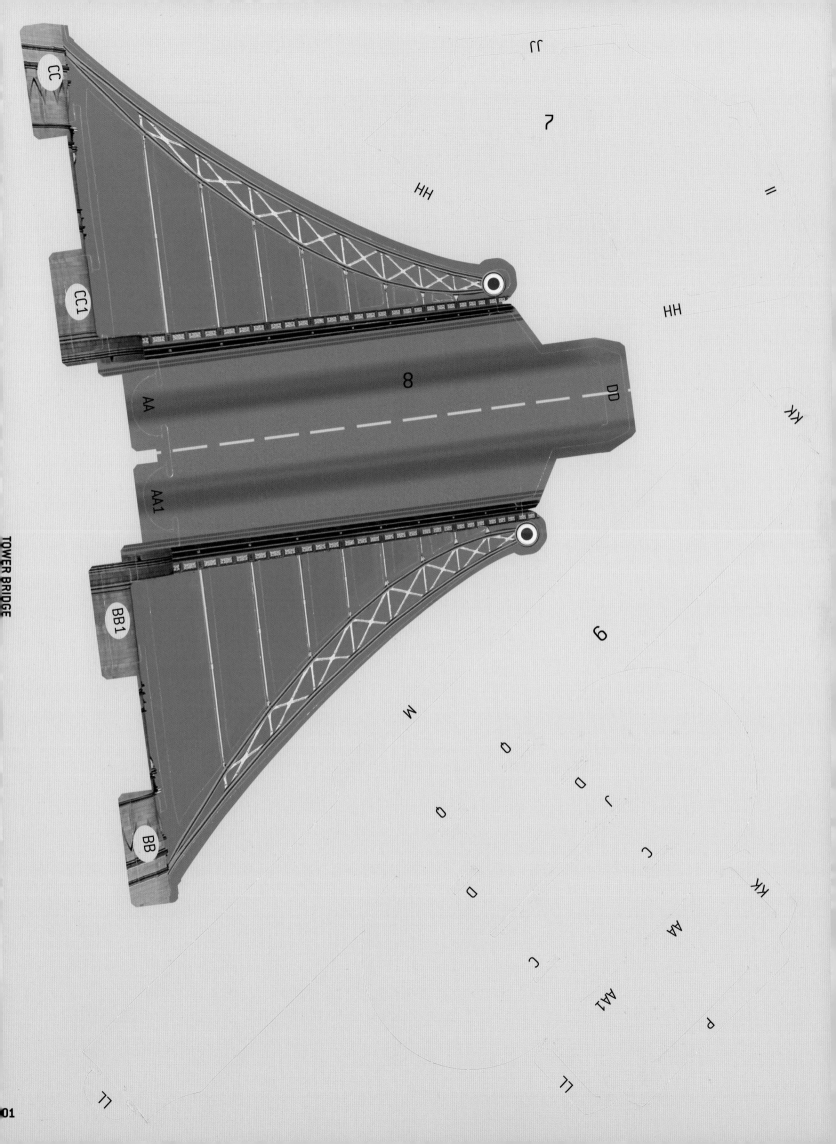

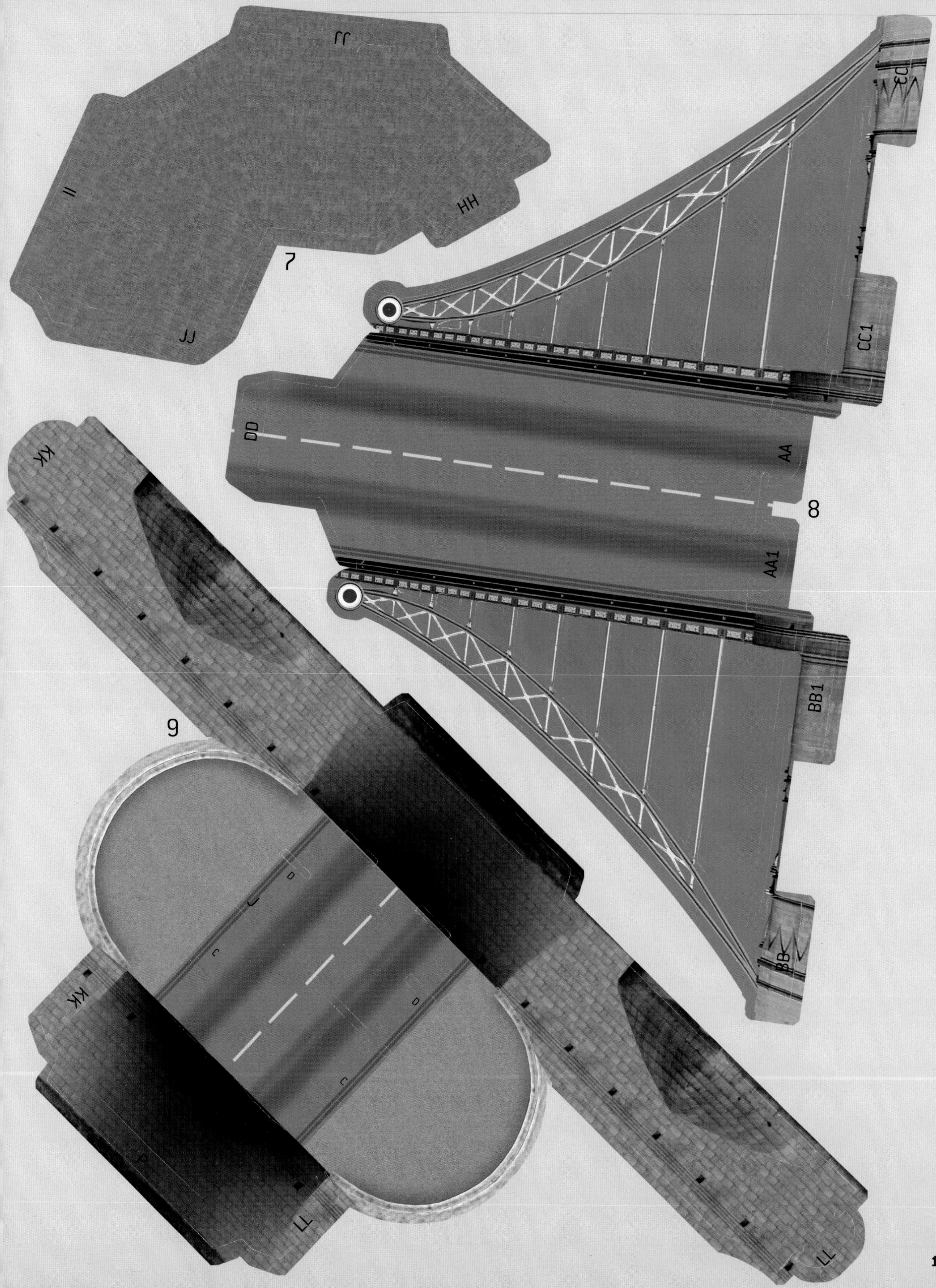

7

II

JJ

JJ

HH

DD

AA

CC1

8

AA1

BB1

9

KK

KK

C

C

D

D

P

LL

LL

BB

CC

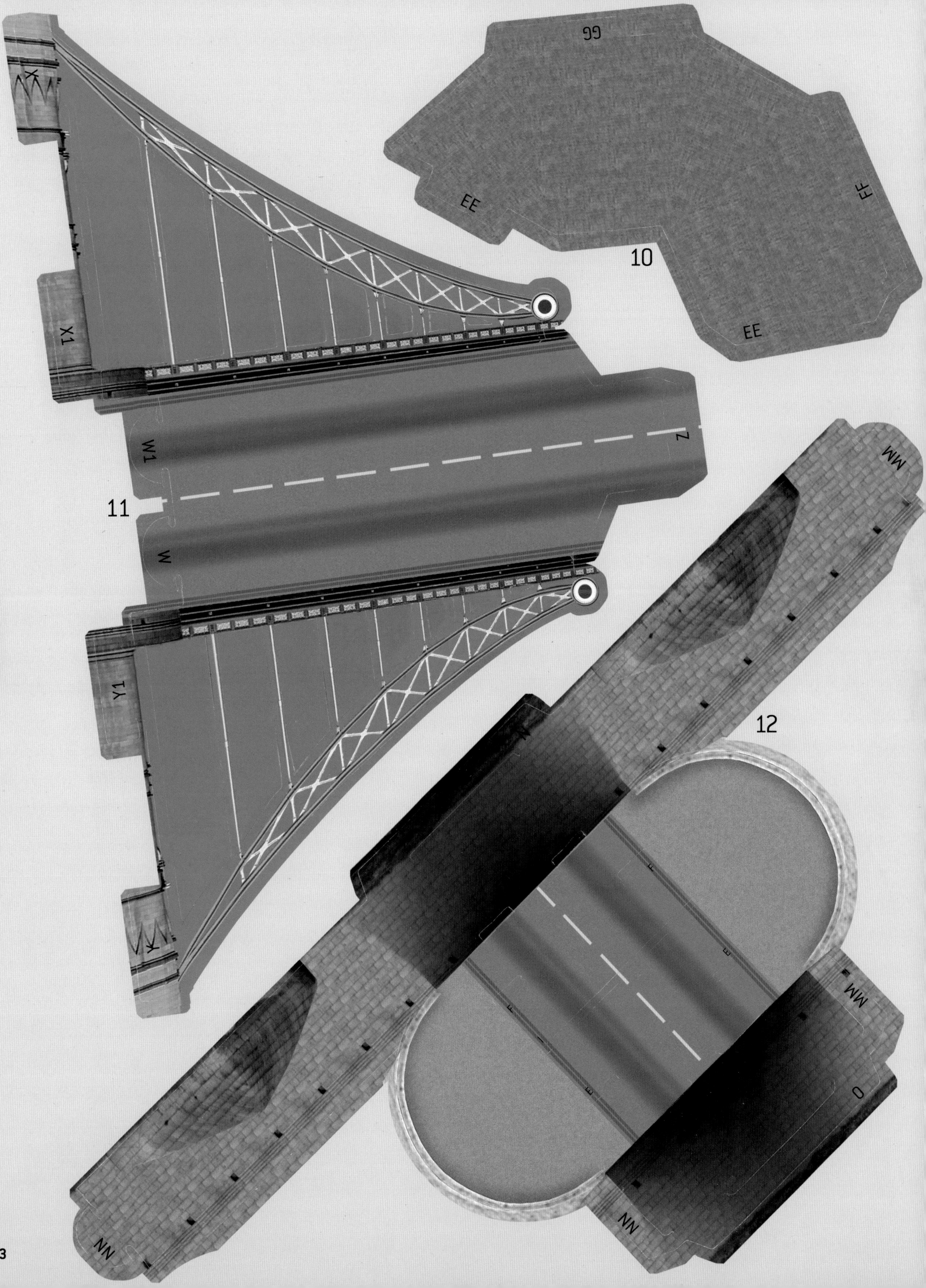
GG
EE
FF
EE
10
X
X1
W1
Z
11
W
Y1
Y
MM
12
MM
O
NN
NN

GG

10

FF

EE

EE

MM

Z

11

W1

W

MM

12

N

R

F

R

E

F

I

W

E

W

O

NN

NN

X

X1

Y1

Y

NN

13

G1

M

P

G

DD

14

G

G1

13

G

14

G1

N

Z

H

16

H1

15

H1

O   N

H

Z

H

16

H1